SUPER STUDENT GRUB

Good Housekeeping

SUPER STUDENT GRUB

PAVILION

Published in the United Kingdom in 2014 by
Pavilion
1 Gower Street
London
WC1E 6HD

The expression Good Housekeeping as used in the title of the book is the
trademark of the National Magazine Company and The Hearst Corporation,
registered in the United Kingdom and USA, and other principal countries of the
world, and is the absolute property of The National Magazine Company and
The Hearst Corporation. The use of this trademark other than with the express
permission of The National Magazine Company or The Hearst Corporation is
strictly prohibited.

The Good Housekeeping website is
www.goodhousekeeping.co.uk

10 9 8 7 6 5 4 3 2 1

ISBN 978-1-909397-95-8

A catalogue record for this book is available from
the British Library.

Reproduction by Dot Gradations Ltd, UK
Printed and bound by 1010 Printing International Ltd, China

This book can be ordered direct from the publisher. Contact the marketing
department, but try your bookshop first.

www.pavilionbooks.com

Picture Credits

Photographers:
Neil Barclay (pages 74, 83, 92, 144, 210, 212, 225, 227, 231 and 233); Martin Brigdale (page 162); Nicki Dowey (pages 33, 36, 38, 66, 67, 69, 70, 71, 73, 75, 76, 77, 80, 81, 84, 87, 88, 91, 94, 95, 96, 103, 104, 105, 106, 107, 108, 109, 110, 111, 112, 114, 115, 118, 119, 121, 122,123, 124, 125, 126, 127, 128, 129, 136, 137, 138, 139, 141, 142, 143, 148, 150, 152, 153, 157, 158, 159, 160, 166, 167, 168, 170, 172, 173, 174, 176, 177, 186, 188, 189, 192, 193, 197, 199, 200, 201, 205, 206, 207, 208, 209, 214, 215, 216, 221, 228 and 230); Daniel Jones (page 145); Jonathan Lovekin (page 101); Lis Parsons (pages 82 and 156); Craig Robertson (pages 85, 86, 89, 90, 97, 100, 113, 140, 149, 151, 156, 161, 163, 171, 175, 185, 198, 211, 220, 222, 223, 224, 226, 232 and 235); Lucinda Symons (pages 30, 31, 42, 52, 62, 68, 72, 93, 120, 132, 134, 184, 194, 213 and 217); Elizabeth Zeschin (page 195).

Stylists:
Penny Markham, Wei Tang, Helen Trent, Fanny Ward and Mari Mererid Williams.

Home Economists:
Anna Burges-Lumsden, Joanna Farrow, Emma Jane Frost, Teresa Goldfinch, Alice Hart, Lucy McKelvie, Kim Morphew, Katie Rogers, Bridget Sargeson, Stella Sargeson, Sarah Tildesley, Jennifer White and Mari Mererid Williams.

Notes

Both metric and imperial measures are given for the recipes. Follow either set of meas
not a mixture of both, as they are not interchangeable.
All spoon measures are level.
1 tsp = 5ml spoon; 1 tbsp = 15ml spoon.
Ovens and grills must be preheated to the specified temperature.
Medium eggs should be used except where otherwise specified.

Dietary Guidelines

Note that certain recipes contain raw or lightly cooked eggs. The young, elderly, pregnant
women and anyone with immune-deficiency disease should avoid these because of the slight
risk of salmonella.
Note that some recipes contain alcohol. Check the ingredients list before serving to children.

Contents

KITCHEN SMARTS

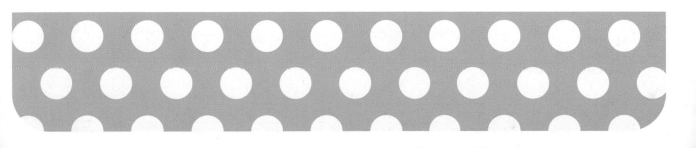

Stuff for the Kitchen

Some student houses or flats come with a few pieces of cooking equipment – and perhaps a microwave – but most don't. Although it's easiest to cook with a variety of good utensils, it's amazing what you can get by without, but there are some essentials that you will certainly have to provide. There's no need to spend lots – cheaper shops have good selections that are fine for your student days. If you can invest in a good cook's knife, however, you will find it's worth the money. Have a look through the Essentials list and see how many things are already in your kitchen and then stock up with the others. Other useful items are also included for the keen cooks.

ESSENTIALS

Pans
❏ **Three saucepans with lids: small, medium and large**
❏ **Large frying pan**

Measuring
❏ **A 600ml (1 pint) measuring jug**
❏ **Measuring spoon**

Cutting, chopping and peeling
❏ **Three cook's knives: one large, one medium and a small serrated knife**
❏ **Bread knife**
❏ **Vegetable peeler**
❏ **Kitchen scissors**
❏ **Two chopping boards: one for vegetables or cooked food and one for raw meat, fish or poultry**

Draining, stirring and transferring
❏ **Large sieve**
❏ **Large plastic spoon**
❏ **Wooden spoons**

Bowls
❏ **Two different sized bowls**

Oven-cooking
❏ **A roasting tin**
❏ **Ovenproof cooking dish**
❏ **Flameproof casserole**

Handy utensils and other items
❏ **Can opener**
❏ **Corkscrew**
❏ **Kettle**
❏ **Tea towels**
❏ **Toaster**

USEFUL TO HAVE

❏ **Kitchen scales**

Baking
❏ **Large mixing bowl**
❏ **20.5cm (8in) cake tin**
❏ **Wire rack**
❏ **Baking parchment**

Stirring and transferring
❏ **Whisk**
❏ **Rubber spatula (particularly if you like to bake)**
❏ **Tongs (handy for turning grilled foods and for serving spaghetti)**

Oven-cooking
❏ **Baking tray**

Handy utensils and other items
❏ **Grater**
❏ **Potato masher**
❏ **Rolling pin**

Electrical equipment
❏ **Stick blender**

BAKING WITHOUT SCALES

As long as you have a tablespoon, you can measure out your baking ingredients without scales:

1 well-heaped tablespoon flour = 25g (1oz)

1 rounded tablespoon sugar = 25g (1oz)

Divide a block of butter in half to estimate 125g (4oz), in half again for 50g (2oz), and again for 25g (1oz)

Stocking Up

If you've got a good basic storecupboard, fridge and freezer you won't be nipping out to the shops every day, but first you need to decide which kinds of foods you like to eat, as this will obviously affect your choices. Look through the lists below to see what you would realistically use in a week, then look through the recipes to see which other ingredients you need to add. Don't get carried away, though. It's easy to stock up on things that never get eaten, especially the perishables. (See page 10 for more about planning your week's shopping.)

STORECUPBOARD BASICS

- ❑ Bread
- ❑ Cans of tomatoes, tuna
- ❑ Curry paste
- ❑ Dried mixed herbs
- ❑ Dried red lentils
- ❑ Mayonnaise
- ❑ Oils (olive, sunflower)
- ❑ Pasta and noodles
- ❑ Peanut butter
- ❑ Pulses (canned): red kidney beans, chickpeas, Puy lentils
- ❑ Basmati rice
- ❑ Salt and pepper
- ❑ Sauces (Worcestershire, soy, Tabasco, sweet chilli)
- ❑ Spices (curry powder, paprika, turmeric)
- ❑ Stock cubes (chicken, beef, vegetable, or vegetable bouillon
- ❑ Sugar (caster)
- ❑ Tea and coffee
- ❑ Tomato ketchup and purée
- ❑ Vinegar (white or red wine)

EXTRAS

- ❑ Chutneys and pickles
- ❑ Cocoa powder
- ❑ Dried fruit (apricots, sultanas, raisins)
- ❑ Dried herbs (oregano, rosemary, thyme, sage, bay leaves)
- ❑ Flour (self-raising, plain)
- ❑ Jam, marmalade and honey
- ❑ Mustard (Dijon, English or wholegrain
- ❑ Pesto
- ❑ Spices (cayenne, cinnamon, nutmeg)
- ❑ Tortilla wraps

FRIDGE

- ❑ Bacon
- ❑ Butter
- ❑ Cheese
- ❑ Eggs
- ❑ Yogurt
- ❑ Milk or soya milk

FREEZER

- ❑ Chicken breasts (frozen singly)
- ❑ Cooked prawns/mixed seafood
- ❑ Peas
- ❑ Sweetcorn

VEGETABLE RACK AND FRUIT BOWL

- ❑ Garlic
- ❑ Onions
- ❑ Potatoes
- ❑ Tomatoes
- ❑ Apples
- ❑ Bananas
- ❑ Lemon
- ❑ Oranges

Living on a Budget

You can eat well without spending a lot of money on food or fuel bills. Sometimes it takes a bit of planning ahead though. At other times it's just about saving any leftovers that you couldn't eat and heating them up for another day. Some of the tastiest suppers are simple, straightforward and cheap; Cottage Pie (see page 172) is one example, and many are quick to prepare – essential for the busy, and usually starving, student.

Six ways to save money

1. Get organised Make your list while you're actually in the house, and not on the road to the shops. Check what basics and staples you need for your storecupboard, fridge and freezer (see page 9).

2. Plan ahead Think about what you fancy eating during the week and add that to your shopping list. It's cheaper to cook for two than one in the long run, so make double the amount for some meals, then cool and freeze half. Pasta sauces, such as Simple Meat Sauce (see page 134), curries, casseroles and bakes can all be doubled up and frozen in this way.

3. Share shopping bills with friends.

4. Shop sensibly Stick to your shopping list and look for special offers.

5. Use up your leftovers Heat up that small portion of pasta sauce leftover from dinner the previous day to make a quick lunch.

6. Check out the market or supermarket at the end of the day and buy some marked-down foods, but only if you need them.

Stretching meals

Meat, poultry and fish can be expensive, but you can save pounds on your food budget and still eat filling, nutritious dishes.

You don't need to buy a giant piece of meat to serve one person. As a rough guide, a chicken breast weighing about 150g (5oz) will serve one; or buy double the weight and use for two meals.

Buy cheaper cuts of meat, such as chicken thighs and sausages. Casseroles and stews usually include plenty of vegetables, so you can just serve with bread if you like. Cook these dishes in bulk to save on fuel and then store in the fridge for up to three days or put in the freezer. Try Braised Meat (page 38) or Easy Chicken & Vegetable Hotpot (page 156).

Add canned beans and pulses to bulk out stews and casseroles, whether made with meat or without. Drain and rinse them first.

Remember that frozen food can be cheaper than fresh, so if you can store it buy it.

Leftover delights

There are plenty of recipes in this book that can be made with typical fridge leftovers:

LEFTOVER	RECIPE
Apples past their best	Express Apple Tart (page 233)
Bacon rashers	Bacon & Egg Salad (page 114), Quick & Easy Carbonara (page 135)
Cooked pasta	Quick Winter Minestrone (page 205), Fast Macaroni Cheese (page 143), Pasta with Pesto & Beans (page 142)
Cooked potatoes	Herring & Potato Salad (page 105)
Custard	Cheat's Chocolate Pots (page 227)
Mixed vegetables	Cheese & Vegetable Bake (page 210), Veggie Curry (page 217)
Pancake batter	Cinnamon Pancakes (page 230)
Pears past their best	Pear & Blackberry Crumble (page 232)
Salad	Bacon & Egg Salad (page 114), Easy Tuna Salad (page 106)
Savoy/white cabbage	Quick Winter Minestrone (page 205), Easy Chicken & Vegetable Hotpot (page 156)
Tomato sauce	Simple Meat Sauce (page 134)

FREEZING LEFTOVERS

If you have a freezer, you can freeze small portions of leftovers if you can't decide what to do with them right now – but don't forget them. It's a good idea to label them with your name, what the food is and a date.

One or two chillies *Halve and deseed them, then freeze. They are easy to chop from frozen.*

Fresh root ginger *Peel then freeze. You can grate the ginger from frozen.*

HOW TO FREEZE

Never put hot or warm food in the freezer, always cool the food thoroughly, then chill in the fridge first. Freeze liquids, stews or soups in a container, or in a bag inside a container. Leave a space of 2.5cm (1in) at the top to allow the food to expand as it freezes. Cover tightly, label and freeze. Once frozen, remove the container and store in the bag.

To freeze meat, poultry and fish, put individual portions of the food in a freezer bag, keeping it flat. Squeeze all the air out so that the bag fits snugly around the food; this avoids 'freezer burn'. Tie or seal the bag securely, label and freeze.

Cheaper Than a Takeaway

Takeaways can be pretty tasty, and there are definitely times when cooking really does seem too much like a chore, but when you're trying to keep costs down (and perhaps aiming to eat healthily as well) it's a good idea to have a think and see what you can make that's just as appealing.

Lunches on the go

Although there's lots of choice for lunch on the high street, the costs can add up. If you make your own lunches you'll save money, and they can taste much better too. Otherwise, use up leftovers in salads, wraps and sandwiches.

Soup

You can't beat a homemade soup for a nutritious and warming meal. What's more, they are cheap to make and perfect for using up leftover vegetables. Try Quick Winter Minestrone (page 205).

Pizza

Rather than buying a takeaway pizza, buy the bases and make your own. Spread some tomato purée or Quick Tomato Sauce (page 132) over the base, then top with whatever you have in the fridge:

- **Throw-it-all-together Naan Pizza (page 94)**
- **Tuna Melt Pizza (page 96)**
- **Garlic Cheese Pizza (page 95)**

Friday night takeaway

Many of us like a takeaway to finish up a long and tiring week, but they are expensive. Make your own takeaway alternative and it will save you money and taste fantastic. It won't take long to cook either; in fact, by the time you've ordered a meal from the local shop and picked it up or had it delivered, you could have whipped up one of these recipes yourself:

- **Chicken Stir-fry with Noodles (page 163)**
- **Spiced Tikka Kebabs (page 128)**
- **Fish & Chips (page 176)**

Desserts

An occasional sweet treat is one of life's pleasures, and homemade desserts can be quick to make. When you're feeling in the mood, try these:

- **Strawberry & Chocolate Muffins (page 222)**
- **Quick Lemon Mousse (page 226)**
- **Quick Chocolate Slices (page 231)**
- **Pear & Blackberry Crumble (page 232)**

HIDDEN SALT

Salt is not good for us in anything but the tiniest quantities, but did you know that three-quarters of all the salt we eat is hidden in processed foods? One small can of chicken soup, for example, can contain well over half the recommended daily intake of salt for an adult, which is 6g (about 1 tsp). That's another reason why home-cooked food is so much better for you. You can add less salt, and even if you have been used to a salty diet, eventually you will have trained your taste buds to enjoy foods with less. Use herbs and spices to enhance the natural flavours of foods and before long you'll be enjoying the real taste of the food – not the flavour of salt.

Eating Healthily

It's the easiest thing to make delicious home-cooked food that is healthy – even when you're cooking on a budget. In fact, some of the healthiest foods are really cheap – take pulses, for example. A can of chickpeas costs pence, yet it can be whizzed up to make a hummus or added to a tomato and vegetable sauce or curry and served with pasta or rice for one of the healthiest meals you could find. Canned fish and cheaper cuts of chicken, such as thighs, make tasty, nourishing meals. Ready-made food, however, generally costs more to buy than fresh ingredients and usually has more salt, sugar and fat than you would add to your homemade version.

What makes a healthy meal?

• As a rough guide, fill about half your plate with plenty of vegetables as a good way of getting your 'five a day'. Always choose a variety, to get a wide range of nutrients. An easy way is to have a leafy green, plus something red or yellow at the least. Your protein portion will then take about a quarter of the plate and your rice or potatoes the other quarter. If you have a pasta dish you might like to eat it with a side salad.
• Always have a small amount of protein: meat, fish, eggs, beans, tofu, Quorn, seeds or nuts. Even if you're not a vegetarian, eat some vegetarian meals in a week. They are cheap and tasty as well as nutritious.
• Eggs, oily fish, unsalted nuts and seeds contain 'essential' fats that your body needs for good health, so eat these regularly every week.
• Dairy foods can make simple and tasty meals. A cheese sauce goes well with vegetables or pasta, or yogurt takes the heat out of a curry.
• Accompany each meal with filling bread, rice, potatoes, pasta or other starchy foods – choose wholegrain varieties whenever you can.

What about labelling?

Although there is a traffic-light scheme developed by the Food Standards Agency to help us know how healthy a food is, the fact remains that if you want to eat well you need to cook as many meals as you can from scratch.

Here are the guidelines for bought foods: a red, amber or green colour coding is given for high, medium or low quantities of calories, sugar, fat, saturated fat and salt. Obviously, green is the one you want to aim for. Guideline Daily Amounts (GDAs) are also listed on foods, and these give an indication of how many calories, fat, salt, sugar and fibre a food contains and what percentage of the total recommended daily intake each of them constitutes (based on 2,000 calories, which is the average requirement for an adult woman).

Use labelling as a guide, if you like, but as a rule of thumb if you stick to buying the food in its most basic state (cans of tomatoes or fish, tubes of tomato purée, fresh or frozen vegetables, fresh meat and poultry, and so on) you'll have more control over what you eat.

TOP TEN TIPS FOR HEALTHY EATING

1. *Enjoy your food.*

2. *Eat a variety of different foods – don't be tempted to stick to the same meals each week.*

3. *Eat the right amount to be a healthy weight. You can check this by using a Body Mass Index (BMI) calculater on the Internet.*

4. *Eat foods rich in carbohydrates and fibre and choose wholegrain cereals if you can. If you're putting on weight, keep carbohydrate portions smaller and increase your vegetables.*

5. *Eat at least five servings of fruit and vegetables each day.*

6. *Keep sugary foods and drinks, and food that is high in fat, as an occasional treat.*

7. *If you drink alcohol, stay within the guidelines: no more than 2 units of alcohol a day for women and no more than 3 units a day for men, with at least one alcohol-free day a week. One unit equals a standard measure of spirits, a half-pint of normal-strength beer or lager, or a small glass of wine.*

8. *Choose reduced- and low-fat dairy products when possible.*

9. *Aim to drink between six and eight glasses of water a day.*

10. *Avoid adding salt to food.*

Your Fridge, Freezer, Microwave and Oven

The fridge

Check the fridge shelves and salad drawer regularly and use up foods before they become inedible. See page 11 for ways to use up odds and ends.

Top ten fridge know-how tips

1. Put all perishable food in the fridge as soon as possible, checking all dates and storage instructions.

2. Wrap or cover all food except most fruit and vegetables, but keep berries covered.

3. Keep pre-packed fresh meat in its original wrapping and use by the date shown. Unwrap freshly bought meat, put on a plate or dish and cover loosely with clingfilm or with a plate or upturned bowl, then put on a low shelf in the fridge. Don't allow it to drip on to other foods. Be especially careful with chicken, which can contain harmful bacteria (see page 16).

4. The coldest shelves are at the bottom of the fridge, so store raw meat, fish and poultry there.

5. To store fish, remove it from its original wrapping, rinse in cold water and pat dry, then cover with clingfilm or with a plate or upturned bowl.

6. Always separate cooked meat and poultry from all raw foods and store it above them.

7. Store cheeses and eggs on the top shelf.

8. Use the salad drawer for leafy and salad vegetables, carrots, courgettes, leeks and cauliflower, and so on, but do not store tomatoes, potatoes and bananas in the fridge, as they do not suit being stored in the cold.

9. Re-cover cream, yogurt and similar dairy foods once opened, as they will absorb other flavours.

10. Cool cooked food to room temperature before putting in the fridge.

The freezer

Apart from storing the obvious frozen foods, you can also freeze sliced bread (toast it from frozen), portions of homemade soup, cartons of fresh soup (reheat from frozen) and bacon (but pack it in single rashers between sheets of baking parchment).

It's essential to allow frozen meat and poultry to thaw completely before cooking, so it's best to take it out of the freezer the night before and leave it in the fridge overnight. Put it on a plate to contain the drips. It will be ready to cook by the time you get home the next day. Cook food as soon as possible after thawing and ensure it's piping hot all the way through after cooking.

Top five freezer know-how tips

1. Put frozen food in the freezer immediately you get home.

2. Freeze fresh food as soon as possible after purchase.

3. Never put warm foods into the freezer, wait until they have cooled, then chill in the fridge first.

4. Do not refreeze food once it has thawed.

5. Freeze raw or cooked food in portions – pack in freezer bags or plastic containers, preferably labelled with name and date.

What not to freeze

Don't try to freeze fried foods (which will go soggy), sauces made with egg, or whole eggs – but you can freeze whites and yolks separately.

The microwave

You can use a microwave for scrambling eggs, cooking ready-prepared meals, vegetables and fish and for softening butter, and reheating foods and drinks. Use any microwave-proof plastic containers (ordinary plastic will buckle), ovenproof glass and ceramic dishes. Shallow, oval or round dishes are best for evenly cooked food. Choose light-coloured containers – dark ones can absorb too much heat, preventing the food from cooking properly.

Top ten microwave know-how tips

1. Don't use metal containers, as the microwaves will bounce off the metal, resulting in food that remains cold. This can also cause damage to the microwave oven.

2. Stir liquid food at least once during cooking, or turn large items of food over.

3. Allow food to rest for a few minutes before eating, to allow the heat to distribute evenly.

4. Cover fatty foods, such as bacon and sausages, with kitchen paper to soak up the fat.

5. Use a plastic trivet to help the underside of the food cook.

6. The microwave oven will work only if the door is closed. The door has a special seal to prevent microwaves, which are dangerous, from escaping.

7. Never switch on the microwave when there is nothing inside – the waves will bounce off the walls of the oven and could damage it.

8. Allow sufficient space around the microwave for ventilation through the air vents.

9. Don't use a microwave for browning meat, cooking puff pastry or breaded or battered foods.

10. Clean the interior and exterior from time to time.

The oven

All ovens cook slightly differently but, generally, fan ovens produce a more even distribution of heat, so they cook food more quickly than conventional ovens. This means you need to adjust the cooking time or temperature for your recipe. The recipes in this book give you an alternative temperature for a fan oven, which is 20°C lower than for a conventional oven.

To cope with spills in the oven, line the bottom with aluminium foil (away from any electric element). Your oven may have a self-cleaning lining but parts will still need cleaning. Clean it occasionally!

Reheating cooked food

When you reheat leftovers it's essential that they are thoroughly heated through and really piping hot. It's the only way to kill any bacteria, so be extra careful. Reheat food once only. Never keep cooked rice warm, as bacteria can develop. Serve it immediately.

TO HELP THE FRIDGE WORK PROPERLY

• *Don't overfill it.*
• *Don't put hot foods in it.*
• *Don't leave the door open.*
• *Keep it clean!*

TO HELP THE FREEZER WORK PROPERLY

• *Keep the freezer as full as possible.*
• *Never add foods that are still warm.*
• *Defrost it occasionally!*

Kitchen Sense

In any student house the kitchen is often a busy place and it's easy for it to become rather mucky and grimy if you don't try to clear up more or less as you go along. Although you don't need to become an obsessive cleaning freak, it's worth knowing some basic rules of food hygiene to keep yourself and your housemates safe.

Keeping the kitchen clean

Thoroughly wipe down work surfaces after use, using clean soapy water. Rinse out the sink daily and wash it properly at least once a week. Don't let pieces of food or fat get washed down the sink, as they can block it – as well as making it smell. Allow fat to cool in the pan before disposing of it.

Empty the bin regularly and wash it out once a week (make sure you don't run out of bin liners). Sweep the floor regularly and wash it once a week. Replace washing-up sponges and brushes frequently and change the tea towels every couple of days; wash them with the washing up cloths at a high temperature. Keep all utensils and equipment clean.

CHICKEN

Raw poultry is the most risky food, because it can contain salmonella bacteria, which causes food poisoning, so take extra care in storing:

• Store pre-wrapped chicken in its original wrapping. Remove fresh chicken from its wrapping and make a note of the use-by date instructions on the label. Cook thoroughly within two days (see page 32).

• Freeze chicken on the day it is purchased. Freeze pre-wrapped chicken in its original wrapping. Remove fresh chicken from the wrapping, then re-wrap in a strong freezer bag, seal and date. It will keep for up to six months.

• To thaw a whole chicken, leave it in its wrapping, place on a large plate and put in the refrigerator for a minimum of 12 hours. Chicken joints will take less time. Use as soon as it has thawed. Never refreeze it once it has thawed.

• After you have prepared chicken, wash your hands and all preparation areas thoroughly, including the sink and especially the taps.

TOP FIVE FOOD PREPARATION TIPS

1. Cleanliness while preparing food is essential, because poor hygiene puts you and others at risk of food poisoning.

2. Always wash your hands with soap, and scrub your nails, before and after handling food, and when handling different types of food.

3. Use one chopping board for raw meat, fish or poultry, and another for vegetables and cooked food.

4. Scrub chopping boards with hot, soapy water, then rinse with very hot, clean water.

5. Never put cooked or ready-to-eat food on a surface that has just had raw meat, chicken or fish on it – wash the surface thoroughly first.

Shopping

It's all too easy to either buy what you don't need or forget to buy what you do need, so it's worth having some kind of routine before you go shopping. Always check your cupboards, fridge and freezer to ensure you stock up on basics that are running low and then give some thought about the week's meals so that you can get a list together of what you'll need.

Remember that there are only so many perishable items that you can actually eat in one week, so don't buy so many that there is little hope of you eating them before the use-by date. Select food carefully and buy it in optimum condition. That means, checking that the packaging is undamaged and that cans are not dented or bulging.

Think differently

One approach to shopping is to do a big supermarket shop once a month for non-perishables (including toiletries and other non-food items) and then buy the fresh ingredients weekly. You might even like to buy some items locally.

Be careful of special offers or BOGOFs (buy one, get one free). You don't always need them but, if you have time to cook in batches or you have space to freeze the extra, they might be useful. Avoid ready-meals and only buy ready-prepared ingredients if they are on a special offer – you'll be paying more for convenience.

Before you go shopping

When you do your quick weekly stocktake of the storecupboard, fridge and freezer, check which ingredients are close to their use-by dates, then think about how they can be incorporated into the menus for the next few days. Look at the recipes in this book and see what you need to buy to make the date-challenged ingredients into something tasty.

Plan your meals for the week
It's well worth having an idea of what you intend to eat for each day of the following week. Include some dishes that you've already made and frozen. Think about meals that might be worth making in bulk – a chicken curry or a pasta sauce, for example. Or make a batch of basic Bolognese sauce and eat half one night then turn the remainder into a chilli with a can of red kidney beans and a few chilli flakes the next night.

Don't forget to include some vegetables and salads to accompany the dishes, but plan to have meals with salad earlier in the week rather than later, as it doesn't last as well as some other vegetables. Bear in mind that you may want to change your plan if you find a bargain in the supermarket.

Rethink your approach to cooking – meat and fish are expensive, so make two nights a week vegetarian.

TOP FIVE SHOPPING TIPS

1. Mostly stick to your shopping list and only buy special offers if you think you'll use them.
2. Buy seasonal foods.
3. If you have a freezer, buy larger amounts of meat or poultry and freeze portions, especially if they are on offer.
4. Compare the price per kilo. Loose fruit and vegetables can cost considerably less than re-packed versions, for example.
5. Don't get carried away with the vegetables and fruit sections – only buy what you need for a week.

MAKE READY-MADE FOODS WORK FOR YOU
The deli counters and canned goods shelves can provide you with the ingredients to whip up instant meals for when you're rushed, but you'll need to shop wisely – some of these items can work out expensive.
• *Buy some good-quality stir-fry, pasta or cook-in sauces. You just need to pop the meat, chicken or prawns in the pan with it and cook it through.*
• *Use ready-baked pastry cases to make a quick flan.*
• *Top a bought pizza base with your own healthy ingredients.*
• *See what the deli counter can offer to go with a salad or to top a pizza: marinated vegetables, cold meats, cured fish and cheeses.*

Get Down to Some Cooking

If you've never followed a recipe before, you'll find it's actually quite easy, because the instructions will take you through step by step. It's worth choosing a simple recipe for your first try, however. A sauce made with meat and vegetables or a curry using a curry paste, for example, are fairly simple for the novice cook.

First things first

• Read the recipe through quickly to make sure you understand it and have enough time to make it. Check how many it serves and amend the quantities accordingly, if the recipe is suitable, if you are cooking for one.

• Check that you have all the necessary ingredients, then make a list of anything that you need to buy (but see the Recipe Shortcuts, opposite). Sometimes you can create a good meal without including every single ingredient listed.

• Check that you have the pans and other equipment.

• Before you start cooking, clear the decks in the kitchen to give yourself room to work.

• If the oven needs to be preheated it will say so in step 1 of the recipe, so do that first.

• The ingredients in a recipe are listed in order of use. It's not necessary to weigh and prepare everything in one go first. You can prepare the onions, say, for the first step and while they're cooking for 5 minutes prepare the next group of vegetables or trim and cube the meat. But if you're cooking a stir-fry you will need to prepare all the ingredients in one go, as it's a very fast cooking method.

• The recipe method will take you through each stage step by step. Take your time at each step before moving on to the next one.

• Use a timer if you have one, or the alarm on your mobile phone – once something is in the oven or bubbling on the hob, it's easy to get distracted and lose track of time.

• Stay in the kitchen while cooking – a pan full of hot fat can be dangerous if it flares up while you've gone walkabout.

• Clear up as you go along.

TOP FIVE RECIPE SHORTCUTS

1. Don't bother with the garnishes.

2. Do use dried herbs instead of fresh if they are being cooked in the dish, but if they are to be added at the end they need to be fresh. Coriander and parsley always need to be fresh, though. (Parsley is cheaper and both herbs can be frozen to avoid waste – dry the leaves, pack into a freezer bag and label. To use, crumble from frozen into the dishes.)

3. If you've only got a green pepper when it should be red, it's OK to use, but the flavour will be slightly different.

4. If you don't have all the vegetables listed, just increase the ones you do have.

5. If you only ever keep mixed herbs, you can use these instead of the specified herb, but the dish won't taste exactly as the recipe – and all your dishes will taste rather similar.

IS IT COOKED?

It's important that food is cooked through thoroughly, especially chicken. Always check that chicken is cooked by cutting it through its thickest part (into the thick part of the leg, if cooking a roast or a chicken portion). The juices should run clear with no pink juices. Beef and lamb can be eaten pink; pork must be cooked through.

Kitchen fires – what to do

Most fires that occur in the kitchen begin when a chip pan or frying pan bursts into flames. Do not leave a pan unattended when frying.

NEVER put water on to fat that is burning; it can cause an explosion.

1. Leave the pan where it is.

2. Turn off the heat, if it is safe to do so.

3. Protect your hands, then put a damp cloth (such as a tea towel), a close-fitting lid or a fire blanket over the pan to smother the flames.

4. Allow the pan to cool for at least 30 minutes. (The fire can start again if the cover is removed too soon.)

Ideally, use a thermostatically controlled deep-fat fryer rather than an ordinary hob-top chip pan, as it is very easy for fat to become too hot and then to burst into flames.

A smoke alarm (to BS 5446) is well worth fitting to the kitchen ceiling or hallway just outside.

THE BASICS

Basic Sauces & Dressings

Gravy

A rich gravy is great served with roast chicken and meat. If possible, make the gravy in the roasting tin after the chicken or meat is cooked and you've taken it out of the tin to rest (this allows the juices to settle and the meat to be tender). This will incorporate the meat juices that have escaped during roasting.

To make 300ml (½ pint):

1. Carefully pour (or skim) off the fat from a corner of the roasting tin, leaving the sediment behind. Put the tin on the hob over a medium heat and pour in 300–450ml (10–15fl oz) vegetable water, or chicken, vegetable or meat stock, as appropriate.

2. Stir thoroughly, scraping up the sediment and boil steadily until the gravy is a rich brown colour.

OR TRY...

Thick gravy
Sprinkle 1–2 tbsp plain flour into the roasting tin and cook, stirring, until browned, then gradually stir in the liquid and cook, stirring, for 2–3 minutes until smooth and slightly thickened.

Sauces

White sauce

Use as a base for lasagne or fish pie, or stir in grated cheese, mustard or herbs and use as a sauce for fish or chicken.

To make 300ml (½ pint), you will need:
15g (½oz) butter
15g (½oz) plain flour
300ml (½ pint) milk
freshly grated nutmeg

1. Melt the butter in a pan, stir in the flour and cook, stirring, for 1 minute until cooked but not coloured. (This is called a roux.)

2. Remove from the heat and gradually pour in the milk, whisking all the time. Season lightly with salt, pepper and nutmeg.

3. Put the pan back on the heat and cook, stirring constantly, until the sauce is thick and smooth. Simmer gently for 2 minutes.

TOP TIP
Quick and easy white sauce
Blend 1 tbsp cornflour with 2 tbsp cold water until smooth. Warm 300ml (½ pint) milk in a pan, then stir in the cornflour mixture. Bring to the boil, stirring constantly for 2–3 minutes to thicken and cook through.

OR TRY...
Cheese sauce
Take the pan off the heat and stir 50g (2oz) finely grated Cheddar or Gruyère cheese and a large pinch of mustard powder or cayenne pepper into the finished sauce. Heat gently to melt the cheese. Use for Cauliflower Cheese or Fast Macaroni Cheese (see pages 208, 143).

Parsley sauce
Stir in 2 tbsp freshly chopped parsley at step 3.

TO MAKE CHEESE SAUCE IN THE MICROWAVE
Pour the milk into a measuring jug or microwaveable bowl. Add the butter and flour and whisk to combine. The butter won't mix in, but don't worry. Microwave on full power (based on a 900W oven) for 2 minutes, then remove and whisk together. Cook for another 2 minutes and whisk again. The sauce should be thick and smooth. Season well, then add the cheese and mustard or pepper and stir until melted.

Salad Dressings

French dressing

1 tsp Dijon mustard
a pinch of sugar
1 tbsp red or white wine vinegar
6 tbsp extra virgin olive oil
salt and ground black pepper

1. Put the mustard, sugar and vinegar into a small bowl and season with salt and pepper. Whisk until well combined, then gradually whisk in the oil until thoroughly combined.

2. Store in a cool place if not using immediately. Whisk briefly before using.

SWAP
Instead of extra virgin olive oil, use olive oil.

OR TRY...
Garlic dressing
Add 1 crushed garlic clove to the dressing with the mustard, sugar and vinegar.

Balsamic dressing
Put 2 tbsp balsamic vinegar and 4 tbsp extra virgin olive oil into a small bowl and whisk to combine. Season with salt and ground black pepper.

Fresh herb dressing
Put ½ tsp Dijon mustard, a pinch of sugar and 1 tbsp lemon juice into a bowl and season with salt and ground black pepper. Whisk until well combined, then gradually whisk in 6 tbsp extra virgin olive oil until thoroughly combined. Stir in 2 tbsp freshly chopped herbs, such as parsley, chives and chervil.

Dijon mustard
Put 2 tbsp white wine vinegar, 4 tbsp olive oil and 1½ tsp Dijon mustard into a small bowl and whisk to combine. Season with salt and ground black pepper.

Eggs

Apart from boiling them whole, eggs need to be either cracked open, separated into whites and yolks, or whisked – and once you have mastered these simple techniques you will be able to cook eggs in lots of different ways.

Cracking and separating

You'll need to separate eggs for some recipes. It's easy, but it requires care. If you're separating more than one egg, break each one into an individual cup. Separating them individually means that if you break one yolk, you won't spoil the whole batch. Keeping the whites yolk-free is particularly important if you need to whisk them.

1. Crack the egg more carefully than usual: right in the middle to make a break between the two halves that is just wide enough to get your thumbnail into.

2. Holding the egg over a bowl with the large end pointing down, carefully lift off the small half. Some of the white will drip and slide into the bowl while the yolk sits in the large end of the shell.

3. Carefully slide the yolk into the smaller end, then back into the large end to allow the remaining white to drop into the bowl. Take care not to break the yolk; even a speck can stop the whites from whisking up.

Whisking

1. Use a hand whisk or electric whisk. Make sure that there is no trace of yolk in the whites and that the whisk and bowl are clean and dry. At a low speed, use the whisk in a small area of the whites until it starts to become foamy.

2. Increase the speed and work the whisk through the whites until glossy and soft rounded peaks form. Do not over-whisk, as the foam will become dry and grainy.

Cooking Eggs

How to fry an egg

1. Crack an egg into a bowl or cup, so that if some of the shell falls in you can scoop it out with a teaspoon.

2. Heat 1 tbsp vegetable or sunflower oil in a non-stick frying pan for 1 minute. If you don't have a non-stick pan use 3 tbsp oil.

3. Turn the heat down low and carefully pour the egg into the hot fat. (If the heat is too high, the white will burn before the yolk is cooked.) Tilt the pan and use a large spoon to scoop fat up and pour it over the yolk – this cooks the yolk at the same time as the white.

4. Cook until the yolk is just set.

How to poach an egg

1. Fill a deep frying pan two-thirds full with water and bring to the boil.

2. Break an egg on to a saucer and slide carefully into the water.

3. Using a large metal spoon, gently roll the egg over two or three times to wrap the white around the yolk. Take the pan off the heat, cover and leave to stand for 3 minutes. Serve immediately. Use a slotted spoon to remove the egg from the pan.

How to boil an egg

Bring a small pan of water to the boil. Once the water is boiling, add a medium egg. For a soft-boiled egg, cook for 6 minutes and for hard-boiled, cook for 10 minutes. Using a slotted spoon, remove the egg from the hot water and serve.

Scrambled eggs

1. Beat 2 medium eggs in a bowl lightly with a fork. Season with salt and ground black pepper.

2. Melt a knob of butter in a small pan over a low heat and pour in the eggs.

3. Start stirring immediately, to break up the lumps as they form and keep the eggs moving while cooking. When they are the consistency you prefer – soft or firmer – remove from the heat.

To scramble eggs in the microwave
Put all the ingredients into a bowl and beat well. Cook at full power for 1 minute (the mixture should be just starting to set around the edges). Beat again. Cook at full power for 2–3 minutes, stirring every 30 seconds, until cooked to your liking.

Baked eggs

1. Preheat the oven – see step 3. Generously smear individual baking dishes or one large baking dish with butter.

2. Put in any accompaniments, if using (see below). If using a vegetable-based accompaniment, use the back of a spoon to make a hollow or hollows in it in which to break the egg or eggs. Carefully crack the egg or eggs into the hollows.

3. Bake for 8–10 minutes at 200°C (180°C fan oven) mark 6, or 15–18 minutes at 180°C (160°C fan oven) mark 4, until the whites are just set; the yolks should still be quite runny.

TOP TIPS
• *Accompaniments must be fully cooked before they are transferred to the baking dish and the raw eggs put on top.*
• *Eggs are delicious baked on top of sautéed vegetables – such as Roasted Ratatouille (see page 211), lightly browned diced potatoes with onions, and well-cooked spinach.*
• *If you like, drizzle a small spoonful of cream and a good grinding of black pepper on top of the eggs before baking.*

Making omelettes

There are numerous different types of omelette – from the folded omelette made from simple beaten eggs to thick omelettes such as Spanish tortilla and Italian frittata.

To serve 1, you will need:
15g (½oz) butter
2 medium eggs, beaten
salt and ground black pepper

1. Add the butter to a preheated small frying pan and let it sizzle for a few moments without browning, then pour in the beaten eggs and stir a few times with a fork.

2. As the omelette begins to stick at the sides of the pan, lift it up and let the uncooked egg run into the gap.

3. When the omelette is nearly set and the underneath is brown, loosen the edges and give the pan a sharp shake to slide the omelette across.

4. Add a filling (such as grated cheese or fried mushrooms) if you like, and fold the far side of the omelette towards you. Tilt the pan to slide the omelette on to the plate and serve.

PERFECT OMELETTES
• *Beat the eggs lightly.*
• *Use a small frying pan – 18cm (7in) is ideal.*
• *Use a high heat.*
• *Don't add butter until the pan is already hot, otherwise it will become overbrown.*

OR TRY...
Ham
Chop 50g (2oz) ham and sprinkle over the eggs as soon as you've added them to the pan.

Herb
Add 1 tsp each finely chopped fresh chives and tarragon, or 1 tbsp chopped freash parsley, to the beaten egg mixture before cooking.

Tomato
Fry 2 skinned and chopped tomatoes in a little butter for 5 minutes or until soft and pulpy. Put in the centre of the omelette before folding.

Cheese
Grate 40g (1½oz) Cheddar cheese. Sprinkle half on the omelette before folding. Sprinkle the rest over the finished omelette.

Mushroom
Thickly slice 50g (2oz) mushrooms and cook in butter until soft. Put in the centre of the omelette before folding.

Making pancakes

**To make 8 pancakes, you
will need:**
125g (4oz) plain flour
a pinch of salt
1 medium egg
300ml (½ pint) milk
oil and butter to fry

1. Sift the flour and salt into
a bowl, make a well in the middle
and whisk in the egg. Work in
the milk, then leave to stand for
20 minutes.

2. Heat a pan and coat lightly with
oil or butter. Pour just a little batter
into the pan and swirl to coat the
bottom of the pan.

3. Cook for 1½–2 minutes until
golden, carefully turning once.
Remove from the pan on to a
warmed plate, and repeat with
the remaining batter.

MONEYSAVER TIP
Use half milk and half water if you don't have enough milk.

Savoury pancake fillings
*Almost any mixture of cooked vegetables, fish or chicken, flavoured with
herbs and moistened with a little soured cream or cream cheese can be
used. Try the following – just spoon on to the pancake, fold over and serve:*

*1. Mix 25g (1oz) each grated cheese and chopped ham with 1 tbsp crème
fraîche (or use mayonnaise).*
2. Roasted Ratatouille (see page 211).
3. Sautéed spinach, pinenuts and feta cheese.
4. Smoked haddock and chopped hard-boiled egg with soured cream.

TOP TIP
*How can I tell if my eggs
are fresh?*
*A fresh egg should feel heavy
in your hand and will sink to the
bottom of the bowl or float on its
side when put into water. Older
eggs, over two weeks old, will
float vertically.*

Cheese

Main types of cheese

Cheddar

Cheddar is a hard English cheese, traditionally made from unpasteurised cow's milk. Smoked versions, including applewood and charnwood, are available. It's good for cooking, as it grates and melts well.

Parmesan

Parmesan is a cooked, pressed cheese with a distinctive flavour that sharpens with age. Parmesan is sold whole or in wedges. Ready-grated Parmesan is a cheaper option but is not as tasty as a piece of the cheese. Parmesan grates and melts well; add the scraped rind to soups, stock or sauces.

Gruyère

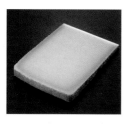

The most famous of Swiss cheeses, Gruyère has a distinctive and fairly sweet taste – at first fruity, then more earthy and nutty. The natural rust-coloured brown rind is hard and dry, the inside is pale yellow, with a dense, compact texture dotted irregularly with pea-sized holes. It's an excellent cooking cheese – use in sauces, bakes, soups and fondues.

Feta

This soft, unpressed fresh Greek cheese is a pure-white rindless cheese, made in blocks using animal rennet, and stored in brine, where it will keep almost indefinitely. It has a sharp, salty taste and a crumbly texture. Use in salads, in pastries and pies or sprinkled on to stews.

Cream cheese

Cream cheese is made from a mixture of cream and pasteurised milk. It has a mildly acid flavour, a rather granular texture, and a buttery consistency that makes it easy to spread. Cream cheese should be eaten shortly after opening or within a day or two of purchase if bought from a large tub. Use as a spread, in baking and desserts, and as a frosting for cakes; and in sauces, savoury dishes and dips.

Mascarpone

Not technically a cheese, as it is made from matured cream, mascarpone is often described as a cream cheese. It has a soft texture, a creamy, mild flavour, and a fat content of 75 per cent. Serve as an alternative to cream with fresh fruit, as a cake filling or topping, or in sauces.

Mozzarella

This fresh cheese, traditionally made from buffalo milk, is now often made with cow's milk. Pasteurised milk is curdled and formed into balls, which are stored in their own water or whey. Older mozzarella, sold in blocks, can be rubbery but melts to form a stringy, chewy cheese, often used on pizzas. Mozzarella should be stored in its own whey or water in the fridge and used within a few days of opening. Use young mozzarella in salads, older mozzarella in pizzas and lasagnes.

Halloumi

Another fresh cheese, this Cypriot cheese is a traditional semi-hard sheep's milk cheese flavoured with mint. It has a milky, salty taste and a rubbery texture. Halloumi is sometimes made with goat's milk or cow's milk. It is always served cooked, usually by grilling, griddling or frying until the exterior is browned and slightly crisped. It is often found in Middle Eastern dishes – cubed and grilled on skewers with slices of vegetables and served with pitta bread and hummus.

Gorgonzola

One of the blue cheeses, this is a creamy-textured Italian cheese. There are two styles: dolce, or nuovo, is soft, creamy and smelly; naturale or piccante is more crumbly, firmer, and stronger in flavour. Use in salads, dips and dressings. In cooking, add to soups, pasta sauces or risottos.

Cooking with cheese

The less cooking cheese has, the better. Overheating tends to make it tough and indigestible, so when making a dish such as cheese sauce, always heat the cheese very gently and do not cook longer than is necessary to melt it. Most hard cheeses are excellent for grating and melting. Soft cheeses won't grate, but can be used baked or melted into sauces. Semi-soft cheeses are excellent for grilling. Blue cheeses are good for melting into sauces, or crumbling into salads. Fresh cheeses such as halloumi (see above) can be sliced and pan-fried, griddled or grilled.

How to choose cheese

Avoid any cheese that has a strong ammonia odour. Hard or semi-hard cheese that has beads of moisture on the surface, or a dry, cracked rind, should be rejected. Semi-soft cheeses should yield to gentle pressure and any powdery bloom on the rind should be evenly coloured and slightly moist.

Buy only as much as you will need (even if it's just a sliver) for consumption within a few days. Refrigeration at home will dry out the cheese.

If buying pre-packed cheese, check that it does not look sweaty or excessively runny and that it is within the life of its date stamp. If the date is many weeks ahead, it may mean that the cheese is immature; this may not matter if you intend to serve the cheese at this immature stage or to store it for using when mature.

Vegetarian cheeses

Some vegetarians prefer to avoid cheeses that have been produced by the traditional method, because this uses animal-derived rennet. Most supermarkets and cheese shops now stock an excellent range of vegetarian cheeses, produced using vegetarian rennet.

Poultry & Meat

Buying and storing chicken

How to freeze and thaw chicken

You can safely freeze fresh uncooked chicken but be sure to follow the guidelines below:

Always freeze poultry before its 'use-by' date, preferably on the day of purchase.

Follow any freezing or thawing instructions given.

Wrap portions in individual freezer bags, seal tightly and label with the date of freezing. They can be stored in the freezer for up to three months.

To thaw, put the poultry in a dish (to catch dripping juices) and leave overnight in the fridge until completely thawed, then cook within 24 hours.

Do not re-freeze thawed poultry. You can, however, freeze it again after you have cooked it.

Most chickens from the butcher or supermarket are sold ready for the oven. Look for birds with no signs of damage or blemishes. If the birds are not wrapped in plastic, check that they smell pleasant. Generally, the larger the bird, the greater proportion of meat to bone there will be – and therefore better value. Check that the birds have a neat shape, an even colour and no bruises or tears on the skin. The body should look meaty and plump.

Some whole birds are bought with a packet of giblets (neck, liver, heart and crop) tucked inside the carcass. Remove and store them in a sealed container in the fridge, to use within a day. Put the bird in a shallow dish, cover with clingfilm and store in the fridge. Use within two days, or according to the 'use-by' date on its label. Poultry from the supermarket can be left in its original packaging.

TOP TIP

Look in the freezer aisle of the supermarket for packs of frozen chicken breasts and thighs. They're usually smaller fillets but cheaper as a result and make a good stand-by.

See page 16 for hygiene notes when handling chicken.

Roasting a chicken

Don't be put off by the idea of roasting – a roasted chicken is easy to cook and very economical.

To serve 4–6, you will need:
1.0kg (4lb) chicken
25g (1oz) butter, softened
2 tbsp olive oil
1 lemon, cut in half
1 small head of garlic, unpeeled,
**   cut in half horizontally**
salt and ground black pepper
roast potatoes (see page 50) and
**   vegetables to serve**

1. Preheat the oven to 220°C (200°C fan oven) mark 7. Put the chicken into a roasting tin just large enough to hold it comfortably. Spread the butter all over the chicken, then drizzle with the oil and season with salt and pepper.

2. Squeeze the lemon juice over the chicken, then put one lemon half inside the chicken. Put the other half and the garlic into the roasting tin.

3. Put the chicken into the oven for 15 minutes, then turn the heat down to 190°C (170°C fan oven)

mark 5 and cook for a further 45 minutes–1 hour until the leg juices run clear when pierced with a sharp knife. Baste from time to time with the pan juices. Add a splash of water to the tin if the juices dry out.

4. Put the chicken on a warm plate, cover with foil and leave to 'rest' for 10 minutes, so that the juices settle back into the meat, making it moist and easier to slice. Mash some of the garlic into the pan juices and serve the gravy with the chicken, with potatoes and vegetables.

TOP TIP
Use any leftover roast chicken in lunches, salads and stir-fries, soups, curries and wraps.

TIMESAVER TIP
Set the alarm on your mobile phone, or use a timer, and let the oven do the work while you get on with other things.

Poaching chicken

This gentle method of cooking will produce a light broth.

1. Brown the bird in oil if you like (this is not necessary but will give a deeper flavour), then transfer to a pan that will hold it easily: a large pan or frying pan is good for pieces, a flameproof casserole for a whole bird.

2. Add 1 roughly peeled and chopped onion, 2 peeled and crushed crushed garlic cloves, 2 peeled and chopped carrots, 2 chopped celery sticks, 6 whole black peppercorns and 1 tsp dried mixed herbs. Pour in just enough stock to cover, then simmer on the hob, uncovered, for 30–40 minutes (for pieces) or about 1 hour (for a whole chicken).

3. Gently lift the bird out of the liquid. If you like, you can increase the heat under the pan to reduce the liquid a little – this will give you a stronger flavoured broth.

INSTANT FLAVOUR IDEAS FOR CHICKEN

Snip bacon into a frying pan, cook until crisp and golden, then stir into warm, boiled new potatoes with shredded cooked roast chicken and mustard mayonnaise. Serve with green salad.

Roast a chicken with lots of tarragon, peppers, whole garlic cloves and olive oil. Serve with couscous, into which you've stirred the roasting juices.

Marinate chicken thighs in olive oil with rosemary, thyme and crushed garlic (see page 45). Pan-fry the chicken thighs (see opposite). Serve with a Quick Tomato Sauce (see page 132).

Pan-frying chicken

This is a quick method for cooking smaller chicken or meat pieces and you can make a sauce with the pan juices at the end, if you like.

1. Put in enough oil to fill a frying pan to a depth of about 5mm (¼in) and put the pan over a medium heat on the hob.

2. Season chicken pieces with salt and ground black pepper, then carefully add to the pan, flesh side down, and fry for 10–15 minutes until it's browned. (Don't put too many pieces of chicken in the pan at once or the chicken will cook partly in its own steam.)

3. Turn the pieces over and cook on the skin side for another 10–15 minutes until the skin is brown and the flesh is cooked, with no pink juices, but still moist all the way through.

4. Remove the chicken from the pan using a pair of tongs and keep warm. Pour off the excess oil from the pan, then add a little stock to the pan and stir to dislodge any bits on the bottom. Stir thoroughly, scraping up the sediment, then add some herbs and finely chopped garlic or onion and cook for a few minutes. Serve the chicken with the sauce.

Grilling chicken

This method is good for cooking tender pieces of chicken, or for strips or chunks threaded on to skewers.

1. Preheat the grill. Brush the chicken pieces with a flavoured oil. Put the pieces on a wire rack over a grill pan or roasting tin and set the pan under the grill so that it is about 8cm (3¼in) from the heat source.

2. Every few minutes brush a teaspoon of the oil over the chicken.

3. When cooked on one side, turn with tongs and cook the other side until cooked through. Avoid piercing the flesh when turning. Allow 12–20 minutes – it is important that chicken is cooked all the way through: pierce with a sharp knife, the juices should run clear.

TOP TIPS

Don't rush the cooking by using a very high heat. If you need to speed things up, cover the pan during the first half of cooking.

Don't let the chicken cook for too long, as it can quickly dry out and toughen over high heat.

Grilling times

Turn the chicken two or three times during cooking.

Kebabs	8–12 minutes
Thighs	10–15 minutes
Breast fillet	10–20 minutes

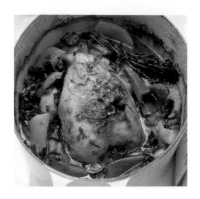

Pot-roasting chicken

Pot-roasting is a great way to cook chicken for when friends come round. There are just a couple of things to watch:

Make sure that you use a large enough casserole and that the bird isn't too close to the sides of the dish.

Check the liquid level in the casserole from time to time. If it's too dry, add a little more. Water is fine; stock or wine is even better.

Pot-roasted chicken

To serve 4–6, you will need:
2 tbsp vegetable oil
1 onion, peeled and cut into wedges
2 rindless streaky bacon rashers,
    chopped
1.4–1.6kg (3–3½lb) chicken
6 carrots, halved
1 garlic clove, peeled and crushed
bouquet garni (see below) or 2 tsp
    dried mixed herbs
600ml (1 pint) chicken stock
    (see Top Tip)
100ml (3½fl oz) dry white wine,
    if you have it
small handful of fresh parsley,
    chopped
salt and ground black pepper

1. Preheat the oven to 200°C (180°C fan oven) mark 6. Heat the oil in a flameproof casserole. Fry the onion and bacon for 5 minutes, then remove from the pan and put on to a plate. Add the chicken to the casserole and brown it all over for 10 minutes, then remove from the pan and put on to the plate. Fry the carrots and garlic for 2 minutes, then add the bacon, onion and chicken.

2. Add the bouquet garni or herbs, stock, wine, if you have it, and season with salt and pepper. Bring to the boil, then transfer to the oven. Cook, basting now and then, for 1 hour 20 minutes or until the juices run clear. Carefully lift out the chicken – tip any liquid inside the bird back into the casserole. Stir the parsley into the liquid and carve the chicken.

Bouquet garni

This is a small bunch of herbs tied together with string, and an essential flavouring for stocks, soups and stews. The herbs can vary but usually include parsley, thyme and bay leaf; spices such as peppercorns and cloves may also be included. You remove it after cooking.

TOP TIP
You can use 1 chicken stock cube dissolved in 600ml (1 pint) boiling water.

TIMESAVER TIP
Set the alarm on your mobile phone, or use a timer, and let the oven do the work while you get on with other things.

Buying and storing meat

When buying meat, always check it carefully first: it should look and smell fresh. The flesh should look moist but not watery, and pink, red or dark red according to variety (mature beef will be dark red). Fat should be pale, creamy and firm – avoid meat where the fat is crumbly, waxy or yellowing. Look for meat that has been well cut and neatly trimmed and remember that some fat will add flavour.

Meat should be wrapped and stored in the fridge, placed in a dish so that if any juices escape they cannot drip and contaminate other foods. Do not allow the meat to touch any other foods. Raw meat can generally be stored for three to five days, although offal and minced or processed meat such as sausages can deteriorate more quickly and should be used within two days. Meat that is bought sealed in a pack can be stored in the fridge unopened, making sure that it is eaten before the 'use-by' date.

TOP TIP

You need smaller quantities when buying cuts of meat off the bone: allow 100–150g (3½–5oz) per person. For meat on the bone, allow slightly more, anything from 175–350g (6–12oz) per person depending on the cut.

How to freeze and thaw meat

You can safely freeze fresh uncooked meat but be sure to follow the guidelines below:

Always freeze meat before its 'use-by' date, preferably on the day of purchase.

Follow any freezing or thawing instructions given.

Wrap portions in individual freezer bags, seal tightly and label with the date of freezing. They can be stored in the freezer for up to three months.

To thaw, put the meat in a dish (to catch any dripping juices) and put in the fridge until completely thawed. Cook within two days.

Do not refreeze raw meat that has thawed. You can, however, freeze it again after you have cooked it.

Braising and pot-roasting meat

Good cuts of beef include shin, chuck, blade, brisket and flank; good cuts of lamb include leg, shoulder, neck, breast and shank; good cuts of pork include shoulder, hand, spring, belly and loin.

Always use a low heat and check regularly to make sure that there is enough liquid to keep the meat from catching on the casserole.

Braises often improve by being cooked in advance and then gently reheated before serving. If you've braised a whole piece of meat, you can slice it before reheating.

Braised meat

To serve 6, you will need:
3 tbsp olive oil
1.1kg (2½lb) meat, cut into large chunks (see Moneysaver Tip)
1 large onion, peeled and thickly sliced
3 carrots, peeled and thickly sliced
3 celery sticks, thickly sliced
2 garlic cloves, peeled and crushed
2 x 400g cans chopped tomatoes
150ml (¼ pint) water or white wine
2 bay leaves
salt and ground black pepper

1. Preheat the oven to 170°C (150°C fan oven) mark 3. Heat the oil in a large flameproof casserole and lightly brown the meat all over, in two or three batches. Remove from the pan and put on to a plate. Add the onion, carrots, celery and garlic to the pan and cook until beginning to colour, then add the meat, tomatoes and water or wine.

2. Stir well, season and add the bay leaves. Bring to the boil, then cover the pan and transfer to the oven for 2 hours or until tender. Skim off any fat.

TIMESAVER TIP
Set the alarm on your mobile phone, or use a timer, and let the oven do the work while you get on with other things.

MONEYSAVER TIP
Meat is expensive, but if you get one of the cheaper cuts – like shin of beef – this will be an economical meal for six of you.

Pan-frying meat

1. Ideal for chops or steaks. Preheat a frying pan and season the meat with salt.

2. Pour in enough vegetable oil to coat the base of the pan. Put in the meat without crowding. Do not move it for at least the first minute of cooking – it may stick.

3. When the meat is well browned, turn and cook on the other side.

Grilling meat

1. Preheat the grill to high while you dry the meat with kitchen paper. Put the meat on a wire rack in the grill pan. If it has not been marinated, salt lightly.

2. Put the grill pan under the heat. Thin cuts should be about 2.5cm (1in) from the heat source, thicker cuts about 7.5cm (3in). Cook according to the table below.

GRILLING TIMES

Cut	Rare	Medium	Well done
Beef fillet	3–5 minutes	6–7 minutes	8–10 minutes
Other beefsteaks	5–6 minutes	8–12 minutes	15–18 minutes
Pork chops/steaks	8–10 minutes	10–14 minutes	
Lamb chops/steaks	8–10 minutes	10–14 minutes	
Lamb cutlets	6–10 minutes	8–12 minutes	

Note
Cooking times are approximate, for a piece of meat 2.5cm (1in) thick.

Fish

Buying and storing fish

For the best results, fish should be as fresh as possible. It's often hard to tell in the supermarket how fresh a piece of fish is but there are some key signs to look for. A really fresh fish will have:

An even covering of scales with no patches and no damage to the fins.

Glossy taut skin.

Bright and clear eyes and bright red gills.

Flesh that feels firm rather than soft and spongy.

Individual fillets should be moist, shiny and plump.

Fillets and steaks should:

Be moist, shiny and plump

Show no signs of dryness or discoloration.

Not look wet, shiny or slimy.

Fish is always best eaten fresh. So store it in the fridge when you get home, and cook it that day.

How to freeze and thaw fish

Fish can be frozen whole or in fillets, cutlets or steaks. Freeze as soon as possible after purchase.

Gut and clean the fish or ask the fishmonger to do this. Pat dry on kitchen paper, then snip off any sharp fins or spikes.

Wrap fish or fillets individually in clingfilm or a freezer bag, making sure the wrapping is airtight. Label with the date and store in the freezer. Use within two to three months.

To thaw, place the fish in the fridge until completely thawed. This may take 24 hours for a large fish.

Do not refreeze thawed raw fish. You can, however, freeze it again after you have cooked it.

Preparing and cooking fish

Whole fish often need to be gutted and cleaned before cooking (except whitebait and red mullet). Those with tough scales should have the scales removed. Small to medium-sized fish can be cooked whole, whereas medium-large fish may be filleted or cut into steaks or chunks. Fillets and steaks may be cooked with the skin on or off, but skin should be removed before cutting the flesh into chunks or cubes. You can ask the fishmonger to clean, scale and skin the fish.

Different fish suit different cooking techniques. The main techniques are steaming, pan-frying, searing, grilling and baking. Fish cooks very quickly, and overcooking will ruin it, so follow the recipe.

Frozen fish

Fish sold frozen is usually snap-frozen shortly after it is caught, and is generally of good quality. It is usually prepared as fillets and is used in processed products, such as fish fingers and fishcakes. Many types of fish and processed foods can be cooked directly from frozen and it will say this on the packet.

Braising fish

For best results:
Choose thick, fairly firm-fleshed fish if you are cooking it in pieces.

You can choose a variety of vegetables and herbs to use in braised dishes: in the recipe below, try adding chopped red pepper and using oregano instead of thyme. Make sure that all the other ingredients are cooked and their flavours well developed before you add the fish.

Once you add the fish to the pan, don't move it about too much, as the flesh can easily break up. Be careful when removing it from the pan.

Braised fish

To serve 4, you will need:
1 tbsp oil
15g (½oz) butter
1 onion, peeled and chopped
2 garlic cloves, peeled and crushed
2 tbsp each freshly chopped
   parsley and thyme
400g can chopped tomatoes
about 900g (2lb) firm-fleshed fish,
   such as pollack, hake and
   whiting

1. Put the oil and butter into a large frying pan and cook the onion and garlic until soft. Add the herbs and tomatoes to the pan and cook until the tomatoes are fairly thick.

2. Put the fish on the vegetables and spoon the tomatoes over it.

3. Cook for 5–10 minutes until the fish is just cooked through.

MONEYSAVER TIP
Make this when you see some cheap fish on sale.

Everyday Fish

Cod

Once plentiful, cod has been over-fished and stocks have dropped to dangerously low levels. Cod is usually available as steaks or fillets. Cod suits simple flavourings such as butter and lemon, or sauces such as parsley or a creamy cheese sauce, as well as Mediterranean flavours. Batter and deep-fry, braise in sauces, poach, grill, bake or roast. Avoid overcooking, as the flesh easily becomes dry or watery.

Pollack

Pollack is a member of the cod family with firm, white, flavoursome flesh. Alhough usually considered inferior to cod and haddock in flavour, its abundance and lower price make it a good alternative. Pollack is usually sold as fillets or cutlets. It goes well with Indian spices such as cumin, coriander and turmeric, as well as Mediterranean flavours. Braise, bake or add to soups, casseroles and fish pies.

Whiting

Whiting is one of the smallest members of the cod family, and has delicately flavoured flesh. It is usually sold whole. Less expensive than cod, it is good cooked with garlic, tomatoes and dill, or a citrus sauce. Pan-fry or grill whole fish. Deep-fry, braise or poach fillets, or add to soups.

Hake

Hake is another member of the cod family, and similarly over-fished. Their flesh is white and fragile with a delicate flavour, and should be cooked with care. Hake is usually available as steaks and cutlets and goes well with garlic and white wine, tomatoes and paprika. Poach, braise, bake or fry.

Mackerel

Mackerel can vary greatly in size but the average fish weighs about 450g (1lb). The flesh is a beige-pink and has a meaty texture and rich flavour. Mackerel are in plentiful supply and inexpensive, and are excellent in terms of price to quality ratio. They are usually sold whole and are best eaten very fresh. Serve well seasoned with pepper and grilled, with just a squeeze of lemon juice, or accompany with a sharp and piquant sauce such as gooseberry, cranberry, rhubarb, mustard or horseradish. Whole fish and fillets can be grilled, baked, pan-fried or braised.

Sardines

Sardines vary in size, with the average fish about 10cm (4in) long. They have a firm, richly flavoured flesh, and are best eaten extremely fresh. They go well with citrus flavours such as lemon and orange, and with tomatoes. But they are particularly tasty when simply brushed with oil (optionally flavoured with garlic, marjoram or thyme) and then barbecued. They have a multitude of fine bones, which can sometimes be eaten but may be pulled off the meat with great care. Allow 3–5 sardines per serving. Cook whole, or fillet, and grill, barbecue or pan-fry and serve with a squeeze of lemon juice.

Canned Fish

A number of common canned fish make useful storecupboard standbys for when you want to make a quick meal.

Tuna
Canned in oil, brine or spring water and available as chunks or steaks, canned tuna has a different texture to fresh. It is pinkish-grey in colour, with a dry and firm texture, and the fish flakes easily. Once opened, store in the fridge and use within two days. Drain all types of tuna. Can be mixed with mayonnaise to use in sandwiches, or use in salads or add to sauces.

Sardines
Whole sardines are gutted, with their heads and tails removed, then canned in oil or tomato sauce. Canning softens the bones, making them edible. Once opened, store in the fridge for up to two days. Drain sardines in oil. Serve on toast, mash to make pâté, or add to pasta sauces.

Pilchards
These fish, which are mature sardines, are usually canned in tomato sauce. Pilchards are canned in the same way as sardines, resulting in soft, edible bones. Once opened, store in the fridge and use within two days. Serve on toast, or add to pasta sauces.

Mackerel
Skinned mackerel fillets are canned in oil, brine or a sauce such as tomato or mustard. They have a firm, meaty texture. Once opened, store in the fridge and use within two days. Drain mackerel in oil or brine. Serve on toast, or add to pasta sauces.

Salmon
Canned salmon is soft and slightly gelatinous. Although it still contains its bones, these are softened by the canning process, making them edible and a good source of calcium. Once opened, store in the fridge and use within two days. Drain and use in fishcakes, pies and sandwiches.

Vegetables

Preparing vegetables

Peeling tomatoes

1. Fill a bowl or pan with boiling water. Using a slotted spoon, add the tomato for 15–30 seconds, then remove to a board.

2. Peel off the skin; it should come away easily depending on ripeness. To remove the seeds, halve the tomato and scoop out the seeds with a spoon or cut out with a small sharp knife.

Seeding peppers

1. Cut the pepper in half vertically and snap out the white pithy core and seeds, Trim away the rest of the white membrane with a knife.

2. Alternatively, cut off the top of the pepper, then cut away and discard the seeds and white pith.

Chopping chillies

1. Cut off the stem and slit the chilli open lengthways. Using the knife, or a spoon, scrape out the seeds and the pith.

2. For diced chilli, cut into thin shreds lengthways, then cut crossways.

TOP TIP

Chillies vary enormously in strength, from quite mild to blisteringly hot, depending on the type of chilli and its ripeness. Taste a small piece first to check it's not too hot for you.

• Be extremely careful when handling chillies not to touch or rub your eyes with your fingers, as they will sting.

• Wash knives immediately after handling chillies for the same reason. Wash hands thoroughly after handling chillies – the volatile oils will sting if accidentally rubbed into your eyes. As a precaution, use rubber gloves when preparing them, if you like.

Garlic

A head of garlic comprises many individual cloves.

1. Break off a clove from the head and put on a chopping board. Place the flat side of a large knife on top of it. Press down firmly on the flat of the blade to crush the clove and break the papery skin.

2. Cut off the base of the clove and slip the garlic out of its skin. It should come away easily.

To crush a garlic clove Put the peeled clove into a garlic press. To crush with a knife: roughly chop the peeled cloves with a pinch of salt.

To slice a garlic clove Using a rocking motion with the knife tip on the board, slice the garlic as thinly as you need.

To shred and chop Holding the slices together, shred them across the slices. Chop the shreds if you need chopped garlic.

Onions

Using a sharp knife, cut the onion in half from tip to base. Peel away all the layers of papery skin and any discoloured layers underneath.

To slice an onion Peel as above, then put one half on the board with the cut surface facing down, and slice across the onion.

To chop an onion To chop an onion, peel as above, then put the flat sides down and make three horizontal cuts from the pointed end almost to the root. Cut along its length six or seven times. Now chop across the width, from pointed end to root, to make dice. Throw away the root.

Carrots

1. Cut off the ends Using a vegetable peeler, peel off the skin and discard. Continue peeling the carrot into ribbon strips.

2. Slicing Cut slices off each of the rounded sides to make four flat surfaces that are stable on the chopping board. Hold steady with one hand and cut lengthways into even slices so they are lying in a flat stack. The stack can then be cut into batons or matchsticks.

3. To dice carrots Turn the stack at right angles and cut through in the opposite direction.

Broccoli

1. Slice off the end of the stalk and cut 1cm (½in) below the florets. Cut the broccoli head in half.

2. Peel the thick, woody skin from the stalks and slice the stalks in half or quarters lengthways. Cut off equal-sized florets with a small knife. If the florets are very large, or if you want them for a stir-fry, you can halve them by cutting lengthways through the stalk and pulling the two halves apart.

Courgettes

Cutting diagonally is ideal for courgettes and other vegetables in a stir-fry. Wash and dry the courgette and trim the base and the stem. Trim off a piece at the base at a 45-degree angle, then repeat with the remaining courgette.

Cauliflower

First cut off the base and remove the outer leaves, then cut out the tough inner core in a cone-shaped piece. Cut off the florets in the same way as for broccoli (above). Don't cut away too much of the stalk or the florets will fall apart.

Mushrooms

Button, white, chestnut and flat mushrooms are all prepared in a similar way.

1. Wipe with a damp cloth or pastry brush to remove any dirt.

2. Button mushrooms: cut off the stalk flush with the cap base. Other mushrooms: cut a thin disc off the end of the stalk and discard. Chop or slice the mushrooms.

Leeks

As some leeks harbour a lot of grit and earth between their leaves, they need careful cleaning. Cut off the root and any tough parts. Make a cut into the leaf end of the leek, about 7.5cm (3in) deep. Hold under the cold tap while separating the cut halves to expose any grit. Wash well, then shake dry. Slice or cut into matchsticks.

Cabbage

The following method is suitable for all cabbages. The crinkly leaved Savoy cabbage may need more washing than other varieties, because its open leaves catch dirt more easily than the tightly packed white and red cabbage.

1. Pick off any of the outer leaves that are dry, tough or discoloured. Cut off the base and, using a small sharp knife, cut out as much as possible of the tough inner core in a single cone-shaped piece. Or you can cut the cabbage in half, from top to bottom, then cut out the core from each half.

2. If you need whole cabbage leaves, peel them off one by one. As you work your way down, you will need to cut out more of the core.

3. If you are cooking the cabbage in wedges, cut it in half lengthways, then cut the pieces into wedges of the required size.

Shredding cabbage

If you want fine shreds, cut the cabbage into quarters before slicing with a large cook's knife.

Avocados

Prepare avocados just before serving because their flesh discolours quickly once exposed to air. Halve the avocado lengthways and twist the two halves apart. Tap the stone with a sharp knife, then twist to remove the stone. Run a knife between the flesh and skin and pull away. Slice the flesh.

Potatoes

How to choose and store potatoes

Look for hard, unblemished potatoes and avoid any that are soft and wrinkled, or with green patches (which can be toxic) or shoots. New potatoes should feel slightly damp and their skins should rub off easily. If you buy potatoes in polythene bags, remove them and put them in a brown paper sack or similar, and store in a cool, dry and dark place, making sure they are not exposed to light. Maincrop potatoes keep well, but new potatoes should be used within a few days of purchase.

Preparing potatoes

Potatoes should be prepared just before you cook them, because their flesh will discolour once cut or peeled. However, you can peel potatoes and keep them covered in water up to 24 hours ahead.

Most of the nutrients in a potato are stored just beneath the skin, so where possible, cook and eat potatoes with the skin on. New potatoes can be scrubbed, or scraped with a knife. You may need to peel maincrop potatoes if you are planning to boil and mash or roast them, although they can be delicious roasted in their skins. To peel, use a sharp vegetable peeler that removes the skin in a thin, even layer.

Cooking vegetables

Boiling

This technique is suitable for most vegetables, but time them carefully as they can disintegrate or turn mushy if overcooked.

1. Prepare the vegetables and put them in plenty of lightly salted cold water.

2. Cover, bring to a boil, then reduce the heat and simmer until cooked. Drain in a colander.

Boiling times
Note: All timings are for peeled vegetables sliced about 2.5cm (1in) thick, except where noted.

Vegetable	Time
Beetroot (whole)	1–2 hours
Carrots	10–20 minutes
Celeriac	20–25 minutes
Corn on the cob	10–15 minutes
Green beans	4–6 minutes
Potatoes	15–20 minutes
Potatoes, new	10 minutes
Salsify	10–20 minutes
Sweet potatoes	10–15 minutes

BOILING TIPS
• *Don't boil very thin pieces of root vegetable – they are more likely to absorb a lot of water and disintegrate.*
• *Small new potatoes are the only type that takes well to boiling whole. Larger ones can start to disintegrate before they are fully cooked.*

Steaming

This is a healthy cooking method, cooking the vegetables until just tender while retaining their nutrients.

1. Put the vegetables in a steamer basket set over a pan of simmering water, being careful that the water does not touch the basket.

2. Cover and cook until the vegetables are just tender.

Steaming times
Note: For soft results, add 2–3 minutes.

Vegetable	Time
Leaf spinach	1–2 minutes
Peas, beans, carrots, cabbage, cauliflower and broccoli florets	about 5 minutes
Root vegetables	5–10 minutes

STEAMING TIPS
• *Use an uncrowded steamer so that air can circulate.*
• *Cut root vegetables into chunks or dice.*
• *Toss the vegetables now and then during steaming.*
• *If steaming frozen vegetables, move them around occasionally.*

Microwaving

1. Cut vegetables into bite-size pieces and put, no more than 12.5cm (5in) deep, into a microwave-proof bowl. Add a splash of water, season and cover with clingfilm. Cook at full power for 2 minutes. Toss, re-cover and cook for 2 minutes more.

2. Continue in 2-minute bursts until cooked al dente (with a little 'bite'). Towards the end of cooking, switch to 1-minute bursts.

Frying

The frying pan should have a thick base to conduct heat evenly. You can fry most things in sunflower oil, but you can also fry in butter; mushrooms taste good this way, but be careful of burning – add a little oil to avoid this.

Shallow-frying

This uses a small amount of fat – about 1cm (½in) – which is heated in the pan over a medium heat. Pieces of food should be of an even size – potato slices, for example. Don't crowd the pan – cook food in batches if necessary.

Deep-frying

This is a quick method that requires a vegetable oil to be heated in a deep pan or deep-fat fryer to a specified temperature. The pan should be no more than half-full and the oil should be brought to temperature gradually. Foods for deep-frying are often coated with batter or breadcrumbs – vegetable fritters, for example. Cook food in small quantities to avoid lowering the temperature of the oil. Never leave a pan unattended when deep-fat frying (see safety advice on page 176).

How to fry an onion

1. For 1 medium onion, heat 1 tbsp vegetable, sunflower or olive oil over a medium heat for 30 seconds.

2. Add the chopped onion to the pan and stir to coat in the oil for 1 minute. Turn the heat down to its lowest setting and cook for at least 15 minutes, stirring regularly to make sure the onion cooks evenly. Don't let the onion burn. Add a splash of water if it looks as if it's going to. The longer onions cook, the softer and more translucent they'll become.

Cooking potatoes

Potatoes are cheap and can be cooked in lots of ways.

Boiled potatoes

Peel old potatoes, scrape new potatoes. Cut large potatoes into even-sized chunks. Put them into a pan with plenty of salted cold water. Cover, bring to the boil, then reduce the heat and simmer until cooked – about 10 minutes for new potatoes, 15–20 minutes for old.

Roast potatoes

To serve 8–10, you will need:
1.8kg (4lb) potatoes, peeled and
**   cut into large chunks**
3 tbsp vegetable oil
75g (3oz) unsalted butter
salt and ground black pepper

1. Preheat the oven to 200°C (180°C fan oven) mark 6. Put the potatoes in a pan of lightly salted water, cover, bring to the boil and simmer for 5–6 minutes. Drain and return to the pan over a low heat. Shake until the potatoes are dry and fluffy.

2. Heat the oil and butter in a roasting tin. Put the potatoes into the tin. Toss in oil and butter and season. Add flavourings such as unpeeled garlic cloves and sprigs of rosemary, if you like. Cook in the oven for 1 hour, turning from time to time until the potatoes are brown and crisp. Adjust the seasoning and serve.

Mashed potatoes

To serve 4, you will need:
900g (2lb) potatoes such as Maris
Piper
125ml (4fl oz) milk
25g (1oz) butter
salt and ground black pepper

1. Peel the potatoes and cut into
even-sized chunks. Boil as above
until just tender, 15–20 minutes.
Test with a small knife. Drain well.

2. Put the potatoes back in the pan
and cover with a clean teatowel for
5 minutes to absorb the steam, or
warm them over a very low heat
until the moisture has evaporated.

3. Pour the milk into a small pan
and bring to the boil. Pour on to
the potatoes with the butter, and
season with salt and pepper.

4. Mash the potatoes until smooth,
light and fluffy.

Perfect mash
Use a potato masher for perfect
mash. Otherwise, use a fork, but
the mash won't be lump-free.
Mashing is also suitable for
parsnips, sweet potatoes and
celeriac.

Chips

1. Peel the potatoes and cut into
chips, then dry on kitchen paper.
Heat vegetable oil in a large pan
or deep-fryer, if you have one,
to 160°C (test by frying a small
cube of bread; it should brown
in 60 seconds). Fry the chips in
batches for 6–7 minutes until soft.
Drain on kitchen paper.

2. Turn up the heat to 190°C
(a cube of bread should brown
in 20 seconds). Return the chips
to the pan and fry until golden
brown. Drain on kitchen paper,
sprinkle with salt and serve.

Pasta & Noodles

Types of pasta

Penne

The name penne means 'quill', and reflects the shape of this pasta: a short hollow tube with the ends cut on the diagonal, like a quill.

To use Cook according to the pack instructions. Serve with smooth, chunky or creamy sauces; cold in salads (drain, toss with oil, and combine when at room temperature with other salad ingredients).

Fusilli

The word fusilli means 'little spindles', and these short spirals of pasta are a very popular shape.

To use Cook according to the pack instructions. Serve with creamy sauces such as walnut, or vegetable sauces such as spinach and tomato; in salads; tossed with a sauce and baked.

Spaghetti

Taking its name from the Italian word spago, meaning 'string', spaghetti is one of the best-known and most commonly found varieties of long pasta. It consists of long, thin, round strands of pasta that vary in length and thickness. Although it is most commonly sold as plain pasta, you can also find coloured and flavoured spaghetti, including spinach and wholewheat.

To use Cook according to the pack instructions. Serve with oil-based sauces such as garlic and olive oil, or tomato sauce.

Lasagne

These flat, rectangular sheets of pasta may be flat or rippled, with straight or ruffled edges, and are designed to be layered with sauce and baked in the oven; a classic lasagne is made with layers of meat ragu sauce and béchamel sauce, although other popular fillings include spinach and ricotta or a chunky vegetable sauce.

To use Cook a few sheets of lasagne at a time according to the pack instructions. Layer alternately with meat or vegetable sauce and béchamel sauce, then bake. Easy-cook lasagne sheets are also available.

Ravioli

A popular and widely available type of pasta, these stuffed pasta squares with a crimped edge may be made from plain, egg or flavoured dough. Stuffings range from classics such as spinach and ricotta or minced meat, to new ideas such as crab, artichoke or pumpkin.

To use Cook according to the pack instructions. Serve with melted butter or herb butter, or with cream or tomato sauces.

Cooking pasta

Overcooked soggy pasta is horrible to eat, so start testing it a minute before the cooking time stated on the pack. Why? Because by the time you've tasted and drained, it will be done.

Use about 1 litre (1¾ pints) of water per 100g (3½oz) of pasta. Filled pasta is the only type of pasta that needs oil in the cooking water – the oil reduces friction, which could tear the wrappers and allow the filling to come out. If the recipe calls for cooking the pasta with a sauce after it has boiled, undercook the pasta slightly when boiling it. Rinse pasta after cooking only if you are going to cool it to use in a salad, then drain well and toss with oil.

Dried pasta

1. Fill a big pan with plenty of water. Cover and bring to a boil, then once it's boiling keep the heat high so that it's constantly boiling. This will stop the pasta sticking together. Add 1 tsp salt to the water.

2. Allow 125g (4oz) pasta per person. Tip the pasta into the boiling water and stir once. If you're using spaghetti, push it into the pan and, as the ends soften, coil them round in the pan to immerse all the spaghetti in the water. Set the timer for 1 minute less than the cooking time stated on the pack and cook uncovered.

3. Check the pasta when the timer goes off. It should be cooked al dente: tender with a little bite at the centre. If it's done, drain well. Otherwise, cook for another 30 seconds and taste again. Drain in a colander.

Fresh pasta

Fresh pasta is cooked in the same way as dried, but for a shorter time. Bring the water to the boil. Add the pasta to the boiling water all at once and stir well. Set the timer for 2 minutes and keep testing every 30 seconds until the pasta is cooked al dente: tender, but with a bite at the centre. Drain in a colander.

TOP TIP
- *Even if your mobile rings, don't be distracted from draining the pasta.*
- *If you leave it in the water for longer, it will turn soggy and can't be rescued. If you're not ready to serve the pasta right away, drain, return it to the pan and add a drizzle of oil to stop it sticking. It will be OK covered for 5–10 minutes.*

Cooking Noodles

Egg (wheat) noodles

These are the most versatile of Asian noodles. Like Italian pasta, they are made from wheat flour, egg and water and are available fresh or dried in various thicknesses.

1. Bring a pan of water to the boil and put the noodles in.

2. Agitate the noodles using chopsticks or a fork to separate them. This can take a minute or even more.

3. Continue boiling for 4–5 minutes until the noodles are cooked al dente: tender but with a little bite in the centre.

4. Drain well and then rinse in cold water and toss with a little oil if you are not using them immediately.

Perfect noodles

Use 50–75g (2–3oz) uncooked noodles per person.

Dried egg noodles are often packed in layers. As a general rule, allow one layer per person for a main dish.

If you plan to re-cook the noodles after the initial boiling or soaking – for example, in a stir-fry – it's best to undercook them slightly.

When cooking a layer, block or nest of noodles, use a pair of forks or chopsticks to untangle the strands from the moment they go into the water.

Glass, cellophane or bean thread noodles

These very thin noodles are made from mung beans; they need only 1 minute in boiling water.

Rice noodles

These may be very fine (rice vermicelli) or thick and flat. Most need no cooking, only soaking in warm or hot water; check the packet instructions, or cover the noodles with freshly boiled water and soak until they are al dente: tender but with a little bite in the centre. Drain well and toss with a little oil if you are not using them immediately.

Rice, Grains & Pulses

Cooking Rice

There are two main types of rice: long grain and short grain. Long-grain rice is the most often used as it is a good accompaniment. Short-grain rice is used for dishes such as risotto and paella and for puddings.

Long-grain rice

1. Use 50–75g (2–3oz) raw rice per person, but measure it by volume 50–75ml (2–2½fl oz). Regular long-grain rice needs no preparation. Put the rice into a pan with a pinch of salt and twice the volume of boiling water (or stock).

2. Bring to the boil. Turn the heat down to low and set the timer for the time stated on the pack. The rice should be al dente: tender with a little bite in the centre.

3. When the rice is cooked, fluff up the grains with a fork.

Thai rice

500g (1lb 2oz) Thai rice
salt
handful of mint leaves

1. Cook the rice and mint in lightly salted boiling water for 10–12 minutes until tender. Drain well and serve.

Stir-frying

Stir-fries can be as simple or as substantial as you feel like making them. They're quick to cook – but you need to have all the ingredients prepared before you start cooking. You can buy ready-prepared stir-fry vegetables, but they will be more expensive than chopping your own. Ensure your wok or pan is very hot before you start cooking and keep the ingredients moving so that they don't stick or burn. Stir-frying is ideal for chicken and tender cuts of meat.

1. Trim off any fat, then cut the poultry or meat into even-sized strips or dice no more than 5mm (¼ in) thick. Heat a wok or large pan until hot and add oil to coat the inside.

2. Add the poultry or meat and cook, stirring constantly, until just done. Remove and put to one side. Cook the other ingredients you are using for the stir-fry, then return the poultry or meat to the pan and cook for 1–2 minutes to heat through.

Stir-fried mixed vegetables

To serve 4, you will need:
450g (1lb) mixed vegetables
   (not starchy ones like potatoes)
1–2 tbsp vegetable oil
2 garlic cloves, peeled and crushed
2 tbsp soy sauce
2 tsp sesame oil

1. Cut the vegetables into even-sized pieces. Heat the oil in a large wok or frying pan until smoking-hot. Add the garlic and cook for a few seconds, then remove and set aside.

2. Add the vegetables to the wok, then toss and stir them. Keep them moving constantly as they cook, which will take 4–5 minutes.

3. When the vegetables are just tender, but still with a slight bite, turn off the heat. Put the garlic back into the wok and stir well. Add the soy sauce and sesame oil, toss and serve.

TOP TIPS FOR STIR-FRYING

• *Cut everything into small pieces of similar size, shape and thickness so that they cook quickly and evenly.*
• *If you're cooking onions or garlic with the vegetables, don't keep them over the high heat for too long or they will burn.*
• *Add liquids towards the end of cooking so that they don't evaporate.*

Herbs & Spices

Herbs

Dried herbs are excellent for adding flavour to cooked dishes, but in most cases fresh herbs have a better flavour than dried. Buy bunches of fresh herbs from the supermarket or greengrocer and store in the fridge, or buy in pots to grow on a sunny windowsill or in window boxes. All fresh herbs freeze well. Buy dried herbs in small quantities and store in an airtight container in a cool, dark place.

Using fresh herbs

Most herbs are the leaf of a flowering plant, and are usually sold with much of the stalk intact. They have to be washed, trimmed and then chopped or torn into pieces suitable for your recipe.

Washing

1. Trim the roots and part of the stalks from the herbs. Immerse in cold water and shake briskly. Leave in the water for a few minutes.

2. Lift out of the water and put in a colander or sieve, then rinse again under the cold tap. Don't pour the herbs and their water into the sieve, because dirt in the water might get caught in the leaves. Leave to drain for a few minutes, then dry thoroughly on kitchen paper or teatowels.

Chopping herbs

1. Trim the herbs by pinching off all but the smallest, most tender stalks. If the herb is one with a woody stalk, such as rosemary or thyme, it may be easier to remove the leaves by rubbing the whole bunch between your hands; the leaves should simply pull off the stems. If the herb has fleshy stalks, such as parsley or coriander, the stalks can be saved to flavour stock or soup. Tie them in a bundle with string for easy removal.

2. If you are chopping the leaves, gather them into a compact ball in one hand, keeping your fist around the ball (but being careful not to crush them).

3. Chop with a large knife, using a rocking motion and letting just a little of the ball out of your fingers at a time.

4. When the herbs are roughly chopped, continue chopping until the pieces are in small shreds or flakes.

Useful Herbs

Parsley

There are two types of this vivid green herb: flat-leafed and curly. Parsley goes particularly well with fish, ham and vegetables and is good in stuffings for poultry, creamy sauces, and herb butters. The strongly flavoured stalks make a good addition to stocks and stews.

Mint

Mint is equally suitable for sweet and savoury dishes and there are numerous varieties each with their own subtly different flavour. It is an essential ingredient in mint sauce and jelly, tabbouleh, and yogurt dips such as tzatziki and raita. Mint can also add its unmistakeable flavour to green salads and rice, as well as couscous salads and sprinkled over Indian and Thai curries, and fragrant Thai stir-fries. Its flavour also goes well with sweet dishes such as fruit salads, and it is an essential ingredient in two famous cocktails: the mojito and the mint julep. With or without alcohol, it adds a refreshing hint of flavour to summer punches and old-fashioned lemonade. Mint tea is made by infusing fresh or dried leaves in boiling water.

Bay leaf

The fresh shiny, dark green leaves of the bay laurel have a strong smell (stronger than that of the more common dried leaves), so only one or two leaves are needed per dish. Bay leaves are a popular addition to meat and tomato sauces, stews and casseroles, and can be used to flavour marinades for meat, poultry and fish. Individual leaves can be threaded between ingredients skewered on to kebabs to give some of their flavour to the meat. A bay leaf can also add a fragrant flavour to stocks and can be infused in hot milk for dishes such as béchamel sauce. To use, rinse in cold water and pat dry with kitchen paper. Pluck off one or two individual leaves. Use whole, then remove before serving.

Rosemary

A robust herb with spiky leaves and a strong, pungent flavour, rosemary is traditionally used to flavour pork or lamb and other meats such as sausages. It is also good used in hearty vegetable and bean stews and stuffings, but should always be used in moderation, as its flavour can easily become overpowering. Rosemary grows well in gardens.

Thyme

Small-leafed thyme, with its strong, aromatic flavour, is popular in Mediterranean cooking. Add to slow-cooked stews and casseroles and cook with meat, chicken and tomatoes. It goes well with mushrooms and makes a good flavouring for pâtés. The most common varieties are garden thyme and lemon thyme. The latter has a more lemony flavour that goes well with fish, chicken and egg dishes, such as frittatas.

Sage

Pale grey-green, velvety sage leaves have a strong, pungent flavour and it's best not to use too many of them – they add a delicious fragrance and flavour. In Italy, sage butter is a standard accompaniment to ravioli. It is also good drizzled over grilled white fish. To make it, fry a few sage leaves in butter for a minute until crisp, then use immediately. The leaves retain their crispness and look good as well as tasting good.

Basil

This herb has an intense aroma and a natural affinity with tomatoes. Although most often associated with Italian and Mediterranean cooking, basil is also widely used in Thai cooking. Tear rather than cut basil leaves: when cut, the edges are likely to turn black. Add to cooked dishes at the last minute.

Dried Spices

Many dried spices should be fried before using to remove any harshness of flavour and to enhance their taste. Whole seeds, such as coriander and cumin, are usually dry-fried (fried without any oil) in a heavy frying pan until they give off a rich aroma, then ground. Ground spices may be fried in oil before adding other ingredients such as vegetables or meat.

Spices tend to lose their flavour and aroma with age, so unless you use up spices very quickly, buy them in small quantities and store in an airtight container in a cool, dark place. Whole spices retain their flavour better than ground ones, so ideally always buy whole spices, such as coriander and cumin seeds, and grind them as required.

Curry Pastes

Indian curry pastes

In authentic Indian cooking, spices are always freshly ground and blended for each dish. The curry powders and pastes available in supermarkets tend to be generic blends of spices for the Western cook. Powders are usually described as mild, medium and hot, depending on how much chilli they contain, and would typically include key flavourings such as cumin, coriander and turmeric. There is more variety in jars of paste, but these tend to be created in terms of popular restaurant dishes such as tikka, dopiaza and jalfrezi.

Thai curry pastes

There are numerous classic paste blends used in Thai cooking, made from wet and dry spices, herbs and aromatics, but the most widely available readymade ones are red and green curry pastes. Others include yellow curry paste, orange curry paste and mussaman curry paste. Red curry paste typically includes red chillies, cumin seeds, coriander seeds, shallots, garlic, galangal, lemongrass, fresh coriander root, peppercorns and shrimp paste, although there are many variations. Green curry paste is similar to red curry paste, and would typically include green chillies and herbs.

Harissa

This spicy red chilli paste is used throughout North Africa but is particularly associated with the cooking of Tunisia and Morocco. A blend of soaked dried chillies, garlic, cumin, coriander, salt and olive oil, harissa is a lively and versatile mix that can be used in most types of savoury dish. Rose harissa is a variation, which is made with the addition of rose petals.

Chinese five-spice powder

A combination of Sichuan peppercorns, cassia, fennel seed, star anise and cloves. This aromatic blend is widely used in Chinese stir-fries and braised dishes, and goes particularly well with duck and meat.

Garam masala

A classic combination of spices used in Indian cooking, this aromatic spice blend is usually added to dishes towards the end of cooking. Combinations and proportions of spices vary, but a typical garam masala could include coriander, cumin, cardamom and black pepper. Other popular ingredients include cinnamon, cloves and ginger.

Ras el hanout

A complex blend of fragrant dried flower petals and dried spices, ras el hanout comes from Morocco, Tunisia and Algeria. Mixtures may vary, but a typical blend might include cardamom, nutmeg, cloves, ginger and black pepper. Lavender and rose petals are also used in some recipes. Tunisian blends tend to be milder, whereas the Moroccan ones are stronger and more pungent. Ras el hanout adds a warming, spicy, fragrant taste and aroma to tagines and soups.

START THE DAY

Porridge with Dried Fruit

Serves 4 • Preparation Time 5 minutes • Cooking Time 5 minutes • Per Serving 280 calories, 6g fat (of which 1g saturates), 49g carbohydrate, 0.2g salt • Easy

200g (7oz) rolled oats

400ml (14fl oz) milk, plus extra to serve

75g (3oz) mixture of chopped ready-to-eat dried figs, apricots and raisins

1. Put the oats into a large pan and add the milk and 400ml (14fl oz) water. Stir in the figs, apricots and raisins and heat gently, stirring until the porridge thickens and the oats are cooked.

2. Divide among four bowls and serve with a splash of milk.

TIMESAVER TIP

If you've got a microwave oven, put the ingredients into a microwave-safe bowl and microwave on full power for 4–5 minutes, stirring frequently. Take out of the microwave and leave the porridge to rest for 2 minutes before serving.

STAR QUALITIES

Ready in under 30 minutes
Quick and easy
Healthy and sustaining

Energy-boosting Muesli

Makes 15 servings • Preparation Time 5 minutes • Per Serving 208 calories, 9g fat (of which trace saturates), 28g carbohydrate, 0g salt • Easy

100g (3½oz) almonds, chopped
500g (1lb 2oz) porridge oats
2 tbsp pumpkin seeds
2 tbsp sunflower seeds
100g (3½oz) ready-to-eat dried apricots, chopped

1. To toast the almonds, put them into a dry frying pan and heat gently for a few minutes, stirring occasionally, until they start to brown. Don't leave them – they burn quickly. Take them off the heat – they will continue to brown as they cool.

2. Mix together the oats, almonds, seeds and apricots. Store in a sealable container for up to one month. Serve with milk or yogurt.

STAR QUALITIES
Ready in under 30 minutes
Healthy and sustaining
Make in advance

Apple & Almond Yogurt

Serves 4 • Preparation Time 5 minutes, plus overnight chilling • Per Serving 192 calories, 8g fat (of which 1g saturates), 22g carbohydrate, 0.3g salt • Easy

500g (1lb 2oz) natural yogurt
50g (2oz) each flaked almonds and sultanas
2 apples

1. Put the yogurt into a bowl and add the flaked almonds and sultanas.

2. Grate the apples, add to the bowl and mix together. Chill in the fridge overnight. Use as a topping for breakfast cereal or serve as a snack.

SWAP
Use pears instead of apples. Replace the sultanas with dried cranberries.

STAR QUALITIES
Ready in under 30 minutes
Quick and easy
Healthy choice

Toasted Oats with Berries

Makes 4 servings of oats, recipe serves 1 • Preparation Time 10 minutes, plus cooling • Cooking Time 5–10 minutes
Per Serving 327 calories, 15g fat (of which 3g saturates), 44g carbohydrate, 0.1g salt • Easy

**25g (1oz) hazelnuts, roughly
  chopped**
125g (4oz) rolled oats
1 tbsp olive oil
25g (1oz) strawberries, sliced
50g (2oz) blueberries
4 tbsp Greek yogurt
½ tbsp clear honey

1. Preheat the grill to medium. Put the hazelnuts into a bowl with the oats. Drizzle with the oil, mix well, then spread out on a baking sheet. Toast the oat mixture for 5–10 minutes until it starts to crisp up. Remove from the heat and set aside to cool. Store in an airtight container – it will keep for up to a week.

2. To serve, put the strawberries into a large bowl with the blueberries and yogurt. Stir in a quarter of the oats and hazelnuts, drizzle with the honey and serve immediately.

SWAP
Use a mixture of raspberries, blackberries or chopped nectarines or peaches instead of the strawberries and blueberries.

STAR QUALITIES
*Ready in under 30 minutes
Healthy choice
Make in advance*

Apple Compôte

Serves 2 • Preparation Time 10 minutes, plus chilling • Cooking Time 5 minutes • Per Serving 188 calories, 7g fat (of which 1g saturates), 29g carbohydrate, 0g salt • Easy

250g (9oz) cooking apples, peeled, cored and chopped
juice of ½ lemon
1 tbsp golden caster sugar
ground cinnamon
raisins, chopped almonds and natural yogurt to serve

1. Put the apples into a pan with the lemon juice, sugar and 2 tbsp cold water. Cook gently for 5 minutes or until soft.

2. Sprinkle a little ground cinnamon over the top and chill. It will keep for up to three days.

3. Serve with the raisins, chopped almonds and yogurt.

TIMESAVER TIP
If you've got a microwave oven, put the apples, lemon juice, sugar and water into a microwave-safe bowl, cover loosely with clingfilm and cook on full power in a 850W microwave for 4 minutes until the apple is just soft.

STAR QUALITIES
Healthy choice
Make in advance

Breakfast Bruschetta

Serves 4 • Preparation Time 5 minutes • Cooking Time 5 minutes • Per Serving 145 calories, 1g fat (of which trace saturates), 30g carbohydrate, 0.4g salt • Easy

1 ripe banana
250g (9oz) blueberries
200g (7oz) Quark or cream cheese
4 slices bread
1 tbsp clear honey

1. Slice the banana and put into a bowl with the blueberries. Spoon in the Quark or cream cheese and mix well.

2. Toast the slices of bread on both sides, then spread with the blueberry mixture. Drizzle with the honey and serve immediately.

STAR QUALITIES
Ready in under 30 minutes
Quick and easy
Five ingredients or fewer

Cranberry & Mango Smoothie

Serves 2 • Preparation Time 5 minutes • Per Serving 133 calories, 1g fat (of which trace saturates), 29g carbohydrate, 0.2g salt • Easy

**1 ripe mango, stone removed
   (see Top Tip)**
250ml (9fl oz) cranberry juice
150g (5oz) natural yogurt

1. Peel and roughly chop the mango, then put into a bowl with the cranberry juice and use a stick blender to blend for 1 minute.

2. Add the yogurt and blend until smooth, then serve.

TOP TIP
To remove the stone from a mango, cut a slice down one side of the mango close to the stone in the centre. Repeat on the other side. To get the flesh out neatly, cut parallel lines into the flesh of one slice, almost to the skin. Cut another set of lines to cut the flesh into squares. Press on the skin side to turn the fruit inside out, so that the flesh is thrust outwards. Cut off the chunks as close as possible to the skin. Repeat with the other half.

EQUIPMENT ALERT
You'll need a stick blender for this one.

STAR QUALITIES
*Ready in under 30 minutes
Quick and easy
Healthy choice*

Summer Berry Smoothie

Serves 6 • Preparation Time 10 minutes • Per Serving 108 calories, 1g fat (of which trace saturates), 24g carbohydrate, 0.1g salt • Easy

2 large, ripe bananas, about 450g (1lb), peeled and chopped
150g (5oz) natural yogurt
150ml (¼ pint) spring water
500g (1lb 2oz) frozen summer fruits

1. Put the bananas, yogurt and water into a bowl and use a stick blender to whiz until smooth. Add the frozen berries and whiz to a purée.

2. Sieve the mixture, if you like, using the back of a ladle to press it through. Pour into glasses and serve.

SWAP
Fresh strawberries or peaches would taste great instead of the frozen summer fruits.

EQUIPMENT ALERT
You'll need a stick blender for this one.

French Toast

Serves 4 • Preparation Time 5 minutes • Cooking Time 10 minutes • Per Finger 259 calories, 20g fat (of which 9g saturates), 15g carbohydrate, 0.7g salt • Easy

2 medium eggs

150ml (¼ pint) semi-skimmed milk

a generous pinch of freshly grated nutmeg or ground cinnamon

4 slices white bread, or fruit bread, crusts removed and each slice cut into four fingers

50g (2oz) butter

vegetable oil for frying

1 tbsp golden caster sugar

1. Using a fork, beat the eggs, milk and nutmeg or cinnamon together in a shallow dish.

2. Dip the pieces of bread into the mixture, coating them well.

3. Heat half the butter with 1 tbsp oil in a heavy-based frying pan. When the butter is foaming, fry the egg-coated bread pieces in batches, until golden on both sides, adding more butter and oil as needed. Sprinkle with sugar to serve for brunch.

TOP TIPS

Use leftover bread for this tasty brunch dish.

For a savoury version, use white bread and omit the spice and sugar; serve with tomato ketchup, or with bacon and maple syrup.

STAR QUALITIES

Ready in under 30 minutes

Quick and easy

Eggy Bread Sandwiches

Makes 1 sandwich • Preparation Time 5 minutes • Cooking Time 5–7 minutes • Per Serving 515 calories, 28g fat (of which 12g saturates), 39g carbohydrate, 2.7g salt • Easy

2 slices bread
a little Dijon mustard (if you like)
a small piece of Cheddar cheese,
   grated
1 tomato, sliced
1 slice ham
1 medium gg
a little vegetable oil
salt and ground black pepper

1. Spread the slices of bread with a little mustard, if you like, then make a sandwich with the cheese, tomato and ham. Press down on the sandwich.

2. Beat the egg lightly in a shallow dish, then season with salt and pepper. Dip the sandwich into the egg, then turn over to coat on both sides.

3. Heat a little oil in a frying pan until hot. Fry the sandwich, pouring over any remaining egg, for 2–3 minutes on each side until golden.

STAR QUALITIES
Ready in under 30 minutes
Quick and easy

Sunday Brunch Bake

Serves 6 • Preparation Time 15 minutes • Cooking Time about 35 minutes • Per Serving 173 calories, 7g fat (of which 2g saturates), 13g carbohydrate, 0.9g salt • Easy

butter to grease
6 English muffins
1½–2 tbsp wholegrain mustard
6 streaky bacon rashers
12 raw cocktail sausages
600ml (1 pint) semi-skimmed milk
4 large eggs
2 tbsp chives, freshly chopped,
plus extra to garnish (optional)
40g (1½oz) mature Cheddar, grated
a large handful of cherry tomatoes
salt and ground black pepper
baked beans to serve (optional)

1. Preheat the oven to 200°C (180°C fan oven) mark 6. Grease an ovenproof rectangular dish roughly 22 × 33cm (8½ × 13in) and put to one side.

2. Split the muffins in half horizontally and spread the cut sides with mustard. Next, cut each bacon rasher in half to make two shorter pieces. Arrange the muffins, cut side up, and bacon in the dish, then dot around the sausages.

3. In a large jug, mix together the milk, eggs, chives, if you like, and some seasoning. Pour the mixture over the muffins, then sprinkle the grated cheese and cherry tomatoes over the top.

4. Bake for 30–35 minutes until the sausages are golden and the liquid has set. Garnish with chives, if you like, and serve immediately with baked beans, if you like.

Pancakes with Bacon & Syrup

Serves 4 • Preparation Time 20 minutes • Cooking Time 20 minutes • Per Serving 730 calories, 32g fat (of which 13g saturates), 84g carbohydrate, 4g salt • Easy

300g (11oz) self-raising flour
1 tsp baking powder
25g (1oz) caster sugar
2 large eggs
75g (3oz) natural yogurt
300ml (½ pint) semi-skimmed milk
40g (1½oz) butter
12 unsmoked streaky bacon
    rashers
25g (1oz) maple syrup
75g (3oz) golden syrup

1. Preheat the oven to 110°C (90°C fan oven) mark ¼ (for warming). Sift the flour, baking powder and sugar into a large bowl and stir to combine. In a large jug, whisk the eggs, yogurt and milk together until smooth. Using a whisk, gently stir the wet ingredients into the dry ones until just combined (the mixture may be a little lumpy, but don't worry).

2. Heat a knob of the butter in a large frying pan until foaming, then drop large serving spoonfuls of the batter into the pan, spacing them apart (cook in batches). Cook the pancakes for 2–3 minutes until the underside is golden and the tops look dry and bubbly, then flip and cook for another 2–3 minutes until golden. Put the cooked pancakes on a baking tray, cover with foil and keep warm in the oven. Repeat with the remaining batter.

3. Meanwhile, fry the bacon in a large, non-stick frying pan until it is crisp and golden.

4. In a small jug or serving bowl, stir together the maple and golden syrups. Serve the warm pancakes stacked with the bacon, drizzled with the syrup.

STAR QUALITIES
Comfort food

LIGHT BITES
& QUICK FIXES

Garlic Bread

Serves 8 • Preparation Time 5 minutes • Cooking Time 5–6 minutes • Per Serving 400 calories, 20g fat (of which 11g saturates), 50g carbohydrate, 1.6g salt • Easy

1 large crusty loaf
175g (6oz) butter, cubed
3 garlic cloves, peeled and crushed
salt and ground black pepper

1. Preheat the grill. Cut the bread into thick slices.

2. Put the butter and garlic into a small pan and heat gently until melted. Season with salt and pepper.

3. Spoon some of the melted butter on to one side of each slice of bread. Put the slices, buttered side down, on the grill rack. Cook for 1–2 minutes until crisp and golden. Drizzle the uppermost sides with the remaining butter, turn over and cook the other sides. Serve immediately.

STAR QUALITIES
Ready in under 30 minutes
Quick and easy

Posh Beans on Toast

Serves 4 • Preparation Time 5 minutes • Cooking Time 10 minutes • Per Serving 364 calories, 9g fat (of which 2g saturates), 55g carbohydrate, 2.1g salt • Easy

1 tbsp olive oil

2 garlic cloves, peeled and finely sliced

400g can borlotti or cannellini beans, drained and rinsed

400g can chickpeas, drained and rinsed

400g can chopped tomatoes

2 fresh rosemary sprigs or a pinch of dried rosemary

4 slices bread

25g (1oz) freshly grated Parmesan

1. Heat the oil in a pan over a low heat, add the garlic and cook for 1 minute, stirring gently.

2. Add the beans and chickpeas to the pan with the tomatoes and bring to the boil. Strip the leaves from the rosemary, then chop finely and add to the pan. Reduce the heat and simmer for 8–10 minutes until thickened.

3. Meanwhile, toast the bread and put on to plates. Grate the Parmesan into the bean mixture, stir once, then spoon over the bread. Serve immediately.

STAR QUALITIES

Ready in under 30 minutes

Healthy choice

After-the-pub Cheese on Toast

Serves 1 • Preparation Time 5 minutes • Cooking Time 5 minutes • Per Serving 895 calories, 67g fat (of which 31g saturates), 37g carbohydrate, 3.5g salt • Easy

2 slices white or brown bread
2 tbsp mayonnaise
dash of Worcestershire sauce
125g (4oz) Cheddar or Red
   Leicester cheese, grated

1. Preheat the grill to high. Toast the bread on one side, then turn it over.

2. Spread the untoasted side of each slice with mayonnaise and sprinkle a dash of Worcestershire sauce on to each. Scatter the grated cheese over, then cook under the hot grill until golden and bubbling.

STAR QUALITIES
Ready in under 30 minutes
Quick and easy

Toasted Cheese & Ham Sandwich

Makes 2 sandwiches • Preparation Time 5 minutes • Cooking Time 8 minutes • Per Serving 551 calories, 35g fat (of which 22g saturates), 27g carbohydrate, 3.6g salt • Easy

4 slices white bread

butter, softened, to spread, plus extra for frying

Dijon mustard to taste

125g (4oz) cheese (Gruyère is good)

4 slices ham

1. Spread each slice of bread on both sides with the butter. Then spread one side of two slices of bread with a little mustard.

2. Divide the cheese and ham between the two mustard-spread bread slices. Put the other slice of bread on top and press down.

3. Heat a frying pan or griddle with a little butter until hot, then fry the sandwiches for 2–3 minutes on each side until golden and crispy and the cheese starts to melt.

4. Slice in half and serve immediately.

STAR QUALITIES

Ready in under 30 minutes
Quick and easy

Snazzy Cheese on Toast

Serves 2 • Preparation Time 5 minutes • Cooking Time 5 minutes • Per Serving 280 calories, 14g fat (of which 9g saturates), 27g carbohydrate, 1.4g salt • Easy

2 thick slices bread (see Top Tip)
2 tbsp cranberry sauce
75g (3oz) blue cheese (Stilton is good)

1. Preheat the grill. Toast the bread lightly on both sides.

2. Spread one side of each with 1 tbsp cranberry sauce.

3. Crumble the cheese and sprinkle on top of the cranberry sauce.

4. Put each slice under the hot grill until the cheese melts, then eat immediately.

TOP TIP
Granary bread and walnut bread are really good with cheese.

STAR QUALITIES
Ready in under 30 minutes
Quick and easy
Five ingredients or fewer

Tomato Crostini with Feta & Basil

Serves 4 • Preparation Time 20 minutes • Cooking Time 3 minutes • Per Serving 242 calories, 17g fat (of which 3g saturates), 18g carbohydrate, 1.5g salt • Easy

1 small garlic clove, peeled and crushed
3 tbsp freshly chopped basil, plus extra basil leaves to garnish
25g (1oz) pinenuts
2 tbsp extra virgin olive oil
grated zest and juice of 1 lime (see Top Tip)
50g (2oz) feta cheese
4 large tomatoes, thickly sliced
150g tub fresh tomato salsa
50g (2oz) pitted black olives, roughly chopped
4 thick slices bread
salt and ground black pepper

EQUIPMENT ALERT
You'll need a blender for this one.

TOP TIP
Zesting citrus fruit
Orange and lemon zest are important flavourings in many recipes. Most citrus fruit is sprayed with wax and fungicides or pesticides. Unless you buy unwaxed fruit, wash it with a tiny drop of washing up liquid and warm water, then rinse with clean water and dry thoroughly on kitchen paper.

To use a grater, rub the fruit over the grater, using a medium pressure to remove the zest without removing the white pith.
To use a zester, press the blade into the citrus skin and run it along the surface to take off strips of zest.

STAR QUALITIES
Ready in under 30 minutes
Quick and easy
Healthy choice

1. Whiz the garlic, chopped basil, pinenuts, oil, lime zest and juice together in a blender to form a smooth paste (or chop all the ingredients and mix together). Add the feta cheese and blend until smooth, or mash. Thin with 1 tbsp water if necessary. Season with salt and pepper.

2. Put the tomatoes, tomato salsa and olives in a bowl and gently toss them together.

3. Toast the bread. Divide the tomato mixture among the slices of toast and spoon the basil and feta mixture over the top. Garnish with basil leaves and serve.

Fancy Tuna on Toast

Serves 4 • Preparation Time 10 minutes • Cooking Time 3 minutes • Per Serving 346 calories, 14g fat (of which 2g saturates), 38g carbohydrate, 2.8g salt • Easy

- **2 x 185g cans tuna chunks in oil, drained and the oil kept**
- **8 spring onions, chopped**
- **1 yellow pepper, seeded and sliced (see page 44)**
- **20 olives, pitted and halved**
- **1 tbsp white wine vinegar**
- **1 tsp soured cream, plus extra to serve**
- **8 thick slices crusty bread**
- **a handful of rocket (if you like)**

1. Put the tuna into a bowl with the spring onions, yellow pepper and olives.

2. In a separate bowl, whisk 2 tbsp of the reserved tuna oil with the vinegar and soured cream. Toss into the tuna mixture.

3. Toast the bread until golden. Divide the tuna mixture among the slices of toast, then scatter over a handful of rocket, if you like. Serve immediately, with extra soured cream in a small bowl.

TOP TIP
If you want to cut down on the fat, replace the soured cream with fat-free Greek yogurt.

STAR QUALITIES
Ready in under 30 minutes
Quick and easy
Brain food

Sardines on Toast

Serves 4 • Preparation Time 5 minutes • Cooking Time 8–10 minutes • Per Serving 240 calories, 9g fat (of which 2g saturates), 25g carbohydrate, 1.6g salt • Easy

4 slices thick wholemeal bread

2 large tomatoes, sliced

**2 x 120g cans sardines in olive oil,
    drained**

juice of ½ lemon

**small handful of parsley, chopped
    (if you like)**

1. Preheat the grill. Toast the slices of bread on both sides.

2. Divide the tomato slices and the sardines among the toast slices, squeeze the lemon juice over them, then put back under the grill for 2–3 minutes to heat through. Scatter the parsley over the sardines, if you like, and serve immediately.

STAR QUALITIES

Ready in under 30 minutes

Quick and easy

Healthy choice

Tuna Melt

Serves 2 • Preparation Time 5 minutes • Cooking Time 5 minutes • Per Serving 390 calories, 21g fat (of which 8g saturates), 30g carbohydrate, 1.7g salt • Easy

2 slices bread (Granary, sourdough or wholemeal are good for this)
2 tomatoes, sliced
75g (3oz) canned tuna in brine, drained
2 tbsp mayonnaise
50g (2oz) Cheddar or Red Leicester cheese, grated
dash of Worcestershire sauce

1. Preheat the grill. Toast the bread on one side, then turn it over.

2. Divide the sliced tomatoes between the two slices of bread, then add the tuna.

3. Spread the mayonnaise over the tuna and cover with the grated cheese. Sprinkle a dash of Worcestershire sauce on each. Grill until the cheese is golden and bubbling.

SWAP
Instead of tuna use a 120g can of sardines or mackerel.

STAR QUALITIES
Ready in under 30 minutes
Quick and easy
Brain food

Mozzarella Mushrooms on Muffins

Serves 4 • Preparation Time 2–3 minutes • Cooking Time 15–20 minutes • Per Serving 137 calories, 9g fat (of which 5g saturates), 5g carbohydrate, 0.4g salt • Easy

8 large mushrooms
8 slices marinated red pepper
8 fresh basil leaves
150g (5oz) mozzarella, cut into
    8 slices
4 English muffins, halved
salt and ground black pepper
green salad to serve

1. Preheat the oven to 200°C (180°C fan oven) mark 6. Lay the mushrooms side by side in a roasting tin and season with salt and pepper. Top each mushroom with a slice of red pepper and a basil leaf. Lay a slice of mozzarella on top of each mushroom. Season again. Roast in the oven for 15–20 minutes until the mushrooms are tender and the cheese has melted.

2. Meanwhile, toast the muffin halves until golden. Put a mozzarella mushroom on top of each muffin half. Serve immediately with a green salad

STAR QUALITIES
Ready in under 30 minutes

Roast Mushrooms with Pesto

Serves 4 • Preparation Time 5 minutes • Cooking Time 15 minutes • Per Serving 258 calories, 23g fat (of which 6g saturates), 1g carbohydrate, 0.5g salt • Easy

8 large mushrooms
8 tbsp pesto (see Top Tip)
toasted ciabatta, salad and basil
   leaves to serve (optional)

1. Preheat the oven to 200°C (180°C fan oven) mark 6. Put the mushrooms into an ovenproof dish, then spoon 1 tbsp pesto on top of each one.

2. Pour 150ml (¼ pint) boiling water into the dish, then cook in the oven for 15 minutes or until the mushrooms are soft and the topping is hot. Serve with toasted ciabatta and salad and, if you like, scatter a few small basil leaves over the top.

TOP TIP
Pesto is a sauce made with basil, Parmesan, pinenuts, olive oil and salt and pepper. You can buy it in the supermarket. Not all pestos are vegetarian, however, so check the label.

STAR QUALITIES
Ready in under 30 minutes
Five ingredients or fewer
Brain food

Veggie Pitta

Makes 1 • Preparation Time 8 minutes • Per Serving 322 calories, 11g fat (of which 2g saturates), 47g carbohydrate, 1.2g salt • Easy

1 wholemeal pitta bread
1 tbsp hummus, plus extra to serve
15g (½oz) unsalted cashew nuts
2 mushrooms, finely sliced
¼ cucumber, chopped
watercress or mixed salad leaves
ground black pepper

1. Split the pitta bread and spread with the hummus.

2. Fill the pitta with the cashew nuts, mushrooms, cucumber and a generous helping of fresh watercress or mixed salad leaves. Serve with extra hummus if you like, and season with pepper.

MONEYSAVER TIP
Use the remaining cucumber for: Easy Tuna Salad (see page 106) or wrap and store in the fridge.

STAR QUALITIES
*Ready in under 30 minutes
Quick and easy
Handy for packed lunches*

Easy Wrap

Makes 4 • Preparation Time 10 minutes • Per Serving 269 calories, 16g fat (of which 3g saturates),
17g carbohydrate, 1.7g salt • Easy

1 tsp salt
1 tsp ground black pepper
2 cooked chicken breasts, about
    125g (4oz) each, cut into bite-size
    pieces
1 carrot, grated
1 avocado, halved, stoned, peeled
    and chopped (see page 47)
small handful of rocket
juice of 1½ lemons
3 tbsp mayonnaise
4 flour tortillas

1. Mix the salt with the pepper in a large bowl. Add the chicken, carrot, avocado and rocket, and mix well.

2. In a separate bowl, mix the lemon juice with the mayonnaise, then spread over the tortillas. Divide the chicken mixture among the tortillas, roll up and serve in napkins, if you like.

TOP TIP
Quick cooking method for chicken breasts
Put the chicken on a grill rack and season with salt and pepper. Brush with oil and grill for 8–10 minutes on each side until cooked through and the juices run clear when pierced with a sharp knife.

MONEYSAVER TIP
Use the remaining lemon for: Bacon & Egg Salad (see page 114).

STAR QUALITIES
Ready in under 30 minutes
Quick and easy

Falafel, Rocket & Soured Cream Wrap

Makes 6 • Preparation Time 5 minutes, plus chilling • Per Serving 270 calories, 9g fat (of which 4g saturates), 42g carbohydrate, 0.5g salt • Easy

6 large flour tortillas
200g (7oz) soured cream
100g (3½oz) rocket
a small handful of fresh coriander, chopped
1 celery stick, finely chopped
180g pack ready-made falafel, roughly chopped or crumbled

1. Lay the tortillas on a board and spread each one with a little soured cream.

2. Divide the rocket among the tortillas and sprinkle with coriander, celery and falafel.

3. Roll up as tightly as you can, then wrap each roll in clingfilm and chill for up to 3 hours or until ready to use. To serve, unwrap and cut each wrap into quarters.

MONEYSAVER TIP
Use the remaining celery for: Braised Meat (see page 38) or Easy Tuna Salad (see page 106).

STAR QUALITIES
Ready in under 30 minutes
Quick and easy
Handy for packed lunches

Throw-it-all-together Naan Pizza

Serves 1 • Preparation Time 5 minutes • Cooking Time 7–8 minutes • Per Serving 806 calories, 39g fat (of which 17g saturates), 96g carbohydrate, 5.1g salt • Easy

50g (2oz) cream cheese
1 naan bread
2 tbsp mango chutney
2 slices ham
½ yellow pepper, seeded and cut into strips (see page 44)
a little olive oil

1. Preheat the grill. Spread the cream cheese over the naan bread, then spoon over the mango chutney. Top with the ham and scatter the pepper strips on top.

2. Drizzle with a little olive oil and cook under the hot grill for 7–8 minutes until the pepper is tender.

PIZZA TOPPINGS
Scatter one or two of the following on top of a basic cheese and tomato pizza:
• *Bits of bacon*
• *Rocket leaves*
• *Dried chilli flakes*
• *Capers*
• *Sliced sun-dried tomatoes*
• *Pepperoni slices*
• *Roasted peppers*
• *Sliced mushrooms*

MONEYSAVER TIP
Use the remaining pepper for: Roasted Ratatouille (see page 211).

STAR QUALITIES
Ready in under 30 minutes
Quick and easy
Cheap eat

Garlic Cheese Pizza

Makes 2 pizzas, serves 4 • Preparation Time 15 minutes • Cooking Time 30 minutes • Per Serving 658 calories, 46g fat (of which 12g saturates), 48g carbohydrate, 1.9g salt • Easy

- **2 x 20.5cm (8in) pizza bases**
- **2 x 150g packs light garlic and herb cream cheese**
- **12 whole sun-dried tomatoes, drained from oil and cut into rough pieces**
- **40g (1½oz) pinenuts**
- **12 fresh basil leaves (if you like)**
- **3 tbsp olive oil**

1. Put two baking sheets in the oven on separate shelves and preheat the oven to 220°C (200°C fan oven) mark 7.

2. When the baking sheets have heated up, take them out of the oven (use oven gloves) and put a pizza base on each tray. Crumble the cheese evenly over the two pizza bases and flatten with a knife, then sprinkle the sun-dried tomatoes, pinenuts and basil leaves, if you like, over the cheese. Drizzle with the oil.

3. Put the trays back into the oven and cook for 30 minutes or until pale golden and cooked to the centre. Swap the pizzas around in the oven halfway through cooking so that they cook evenly.

MONEYSAVER TIP
Instead of pinenuts use chopped unsalted cashew nuts or peanuts.

STAR QUALITIES
Comfort food
Share with friends

Tuna Melt Pizza

Serves 4 • Preparation Time 5 minutes • Cooking Time 10–12 minutes • Per Serving 688 calories, 26g fat (of which 9g saturates), 72g carbohydrate, 3.5g salt • Easy

2 large pizza bases
4 tbsp sun-dried tomato pesto
2 x 185g cans tuna, drained
50g can anchovies, drained
** and chopped**
125g (4oz) mature Cheddar
** cheese, grated**
rocket to serve (if you like)

1. Put two baking sheets in the oven on separate shelves and preheat the oven to 220°C (200°C fan oven) mark 7.

2. When the baking sheets have heated up, take them out of the oven (use oven gloves) and put a pizza base on each tray. Spread each pizza base with 2 tbsp sun-dried tomato pesto. Top each with half the tuna, half the anchovies and half the grated cheese. Put back into the oven and cook for 10–12 minutes until the cheese has melted. Sprinkle with rocket to serve, if you like.

MONEYSAVER TIP
Instead of sun-dried tomato pesto use basil pesto.

TRY SOMETHING DIFFERENT
Ham and pineapple
Spread the pizza bases with 4 tbsp tomato pasta sauce. Top with a 225g can drained unsweetened pineapple chunks, 125g (4oz) diced ham and 125g (4oz) grated Gruyère cheese.

STAR QUALITIES
Brain food
Comfort food
Share with friends

Deli Pizza

Serves 4 • Preparation Time 5 minutes • Cooking Time 15 minutes • Per Serving 440 calories, 15g fat (of which 5g saturates), 64g carbohydrate, 2.8g salt • Easy

6 tbsp tomato pizza sauce
2 large pizza bases
100g (3½oz) soft goat's cheese
1 red onion, peeled and finely sliced
100g (3½oz) sunblush tomatoes
100g (3½oz) olives
a handful of fresh basil, roughly torn
green salad to serve

1. Put a large baking sheet on the top shelf of the oven and preheat the oven to 220°C (200°C fan oven) mark 7.

2. Spread a thin layer of the tomato sauce over each of the pizza bases, leaving a 2.5cm (1in) border around the edge. Top with dollops of goat's cheese, then scatter over the red onion, tomatoes and olives.

3. Slide one of the pizzas on to the hot baking sheet and bake for 15 minutes or until golden and crisp. Repeat with the second pizza base. Scatter the torn basil over and serve with salad.

SWAP
Try marinated peppers, artichokes or chargrilled aubergines instead of the olives and sunblush tomatoes.

STAR QUALITIES
Ready in under 30 minutes
Quick and easy
Share with friends

SALADS

Mixed Leaf Salad

Serves 8 • Preparation Time 10 minutes • Per Serving 112 calories, 11g fat (of which 2g saturates), 2g carbohydrate, 0.1g salt • Easy

3 round lettuce hearts, roughly shredded

100g (3½oz) watercress

2 ripe avocados, halved, stoned, peeled and roughly chopped (see page 47)

1 box salad cress, chopped

100g (3½oz) sugarsnap peas, roughly sliced

4 tbsp French Dressing (see page 24)

1. Put the lettuce hearts into a bowl and add the watercress, avocados, salad cress and sugarsnap peas. Pour the dressing over the salad and toss to mix; serve immediately.

STAR QUALITIES

Ready in under 30 minutes

Quick and easy

Healthy choice

Simple Tomato Salad

Serves 6 • Preparation Time 15 minutes • Per Serving 39 calories, 2g fat (of which trace saturates), 4g carbohydrate, 0.6g salt • Easy

8 medium-size tomatoes
golden caster sugar
1 tbsp extra virgin olive oil
salt and ground black pepper
toasted bread to serve

1. Slice the tomatoes and arrange on a plate. Sprinkle with a pinch of sugar and season with salt and pepper. Leave for 20 minutes to allow the seasonings to draw out the juices.

2. Drizzle with the oil and serve with toasted bread.

STAR QUALITIES
Ready in under 30 minutes
Quick and easy
Healthy choice

Potato Salad

Serves 4 • Preparation Time 10 minutes • Cooking Time 15–20 minutes • Per Serving 335 calories, 26g fat (of which 6g saturates), 24g carbohydrate, 0.3g salt • Easy

550g (1¼lb) new potatoes
6 tbsp mayonnaise
2 tbsp crème fraîche (see Moneysaver Tips)
2 tbsp white wine vinegar
2 shallots, finely chopped (see Moneysaver Tips)
4 tbsp chopped gherkins (if you like)
2 tbsp olive oil
salt and ground black pepper

1. Cook the potatoes in a pan of lightly salted boiling water for 15–20 minutes until tender. Drain, leave to cool slightly, then chop.

2. Mix together the mayonnaise, crème fraîche, vinegar, shallots, gherkins, if you like, and oil. Season with salt and pepper and mix with the potatoes. Leave to cool, then chill until ready to serve.

MONEYSAVER TIPS
Use spring onions instead of shallots.
Use 8 tbsp mayonnaise instead of crème fraîche.

STAR QUALITIES
Comfort food
Share with friends
Make in advance

Easy Bulgur Wheat Salad

Serves 2 • Preparation Time 10 minutes • Cooking Time 10 minutes • Per Serving 399 calories, 6g fat (of which 1g saturates), 77g carbohydrate, 0.7g salt • Easy

**200g (7oz) bulgur wheat
(see page 58 and Timesaver Tip)**
**3 tbsp each freshly chopped mint
and parsley**
juice of 1 lemon
**1 tbsp roughly chopped pistachio
nuts**
salt and ground black pepper

1. Cook the bulgur wheat according to the pack instructions. Leave to cool slightly.

2. Stir in the herbs, lemon juice and nuts and season with salt and pepper. Serve.

TIMESAVER TIP
Use couscous instead of bulgur wheat. Soak it in boiling water for 5–10 minutes.

STAR QUALITIES
*Ready in under 30 minutes
Quick and easy
Healthy and sustaining*

Easy Coleslaw

Serves 6 • Preparation Time 15 minutes • Per Serving 92 calories, 8g fat (of which 1g saturates), 5g carbohydrate, 0.1g salt • Easy

¼ **each medium red and white cabbage, shredded**

1 carrot, grated

20g (¾oz) flat-leafed parsley, finely chopped

FOR THE DRESSING

1½ tbsp red wine vinegar

4 tbsp olive oil

½ tsp Dijon mustard

salt and ground black pepper

1. To make the dressing, put the vinegar into a small bowl, add the oil and mustard, season well with salt and pepper and mix well.

2. Put the cabbage and carrot into a large bowl and toss to mix well. Add the parsley.

3. Mix the dressing again, pour over the cabbage mixture and toss well to coat.

MONEYSAVER TIPS

Instead of red cabbage, use all white cabbage.
Any mustard can be used instead of the Dijon, but if using English mustard you will need only ½ tsp, as it's stronger.
Use the remaining cabbage for: Bubble & Squeak Cakes (see page 194), Buttered Cabbage (see page 195), or Quick Winter Minestrone, (see page 205).

STAR QUALITIES

Ready in under 30 minutes
Quick and easy
Healthy choice

Herring & Potato Salad

Serves 4 • Preparation Time 15 minutes • Cooking Time 15–20 minutes • Per Serving 610 calories, 33g fat (of which 4g saturates), 54g carbohydrate, 2.9g salt • Easy

1kg (2¼lb) new potatoes, scrubbed

8 gherkins, thinly sliced

2 x 280g tubs sweet cured herrings, drained and sliced into 2cm (¾in) strips

FOR THE SOURED CREAM DRESSING

2 tbsp soured cream (see Moneysaver Tip)

6 tbsp mayonnaise

2 tbsp freshly chopped dill

salt and ground black pepper

1. Put the potatoes into a pan of cold water, bring to the boil and cook for 15–20 minutes until tender. Drain, then cut in half.

2. Meanwhile, make the dressing. Mix the soured cream, mayonnaise and dill together in a large bowl. Season well with salt and pepper.

3. Put the potatoes, gherkins and herrings into a bowl with the dressing and toss together. Check the seasoning and serve.

MONEYSAVER TIP

Instead of soured cream, increase the amount of mayonnaise to 8 tbsp.

STAR QUALITIES

Brain food
Share with friends

Easy Tuna Salad

Serves 2 • Preparation Time 10 minutes • Per Serving 313 calories, 8g fat (of which 1g saturates), 35g carbohydrate, 2.1g salt • Easy

400g can mixed beans, drained and rinsed
125g (4oz) tuna, flaked
½ cucumber, chopped
1 red onion, peeled and finely sliced
2 ripe tomatoes, chopped
2 celery sticks, chopped
handful of baby spinach leaves (see Top Tip)
1 tbsp olive oil
2 tsp red wine vinegar
salt and ground black pepper

1. Put the beans into a bowl and add the tuna, cucumber, red onion, tomatoes, celery and spinach.

2. Mix together the oil and vinegar, season with salt and pepper, then toss through the bean mix and serve.

MONEYSAVER TIP
Instead of spinach leaves, use lettuce or salad leaves.

TOP TIP
If you want to make this salad for a packed lunch, add the cucumber and leaves at the last minute. They won't be as crisp when you eat them as when the salad is freshly made but it will still taste good.

MONEYSAVER TIP
Use the remaining cucumber for: Veggie Pitta (see page 91).

STAR QUALITIES
Ready in under 30 minutes
Quick and easy
Cheap eat

Tuna, Bean & Red Onion Salad

Serves 4 • Preparation Time 5 minutes • Per Serving 190 calories, 6g fat (of which 1g saturates), 15g carbohydrate, 1.1g salt • Easy

400g can cannellini beans, drained and rinsed

1 small red onion, peeled and very finely sliced

1 tbsp red wine vinegar

225g can tuna steak in oil

2 tbsp freshly chopped parsley

salt and ground black pepper

green salad and crusty bread to serve

1. Put the beans, onion slices and vinegar into a bowl, season with a little salt and mix well. Add the tuna with its oil, breaking the fish into large flakes.

2. Add half the chopped parsley and season generously with black pepper. Toss the salad, then scatter the remaining parsley over the top. Serve with a green salad and plenty of warm crusty bread.

STAR QUALITIES

Ready in under 30 minutes

Quick and easy

Healthy and sustaining

Greek Pasta Salad

Serves 2 • Preparation Time 10 minutes • Cooking Time 10–15 minutes • Per Serving 382 calories, 27g fat (of which 8g saturates), 25g carbohydrate, 2.5g salt • Easy

3 tbsp olive oil
2 tbsp lemon juice
150g (5oz) cooked pasta shapes
   (see page 53), cooled
75g (3oz) feta cheese, crumbled
3 tomatoes, roughly chopped
2 tbsp small pitted black olives
½ cucumber, roughly chopped
1 small red onion, peeled and
   finely sliced
salt and ground black pepper
freshly chopped mint and lemon
   zest (see Top Tip, page 85) to
   garnish (if you like)

1. Mix the oil and lemon juice together in a bowl, then add the pasta, feta cheese, tomatoes, olives, cucumber and onion.

2. Season with salt and pepper and stir to mix, then garnish with chopped mint and lemon zest, if you like, and serve.

MONEYSAVER TIP
*Use the remaining cucumber for:
Veggie Pitta (see page 91) or
Easy Tuna Salad (see page 106),
or wrap and store in the fridge.*

STAR QUALITIES
*Healthy choice
Quick and easy
Handy for packed lunches*

Pasta & Avocado Salad

Serves 2 • Preparation Time 5 minutes • Per Serving 626 calories, 52g fat (of which 10g saturates), 28g carbohydrate, 1.2g salt • Easy

2 tbsp mayonnaise
2 tbsp pesto (see Top Tip, page 90)
2 ripe avocados, halved, stoned, peeled and cut into cubes (see page 47)
225g (8oz) cooked pasta shapes (see page 53), cooled
a few basil leaves (if you like)

1. Mix together the mayonnaise, pesto and avocados, then mix with the pasta. If the dressing is too thick, dilute with a little water (use the pasta cooking water if you have it).

2. Decorate with basil leaves, if you like, and serve.

TOP TIP
If you have any leftover pasta from an evening meal it's always worth saving it to make a pasta salad the next day.

STAR QUALITIES
Ready in under 30 minutes
Quick and easy
Healthy and sustaining

Pasta, Salami & Tapenade Salad

Serves 4 • Preparation Time 5 minutes • Per Serving 332 calories, 20g fat (of which 6g saturates), 28g carbohydrate, 2g salt • Easy

3 x 225g tubs pasta salad in tomato sauce
75g (3oz) pepper salami, shredded
3 tbsp black olive tapenade
3 tbsp freshly chopped chives (see Moneysaver Tip)
salt and ground black pepper

1. Turn the pasta salad into a large bowl and add the salami, tapenade and chives. Toss everything together and season with pepper. Check for seasoning before adding salt – the tapenade may have made the salad salty enough.

2. Pile the salad into a large bowl. If not being served straight away, this salad is best kept in a cool place (but not chilled) until needed.

MONEYSAVER TIP
Instead of chives, use spring onions.

STAR QUALITIES
Ready in under 30 minutes
Quick and easy
Five ingredients or fewer

Red Pepper Pasta Salad

Serves 4 • Preparation Time 10 minutes, plus cooling • Per Serving 275 calories, 18g fat (of which 3g saturates), 26g carbohydrate, 0.2g salt • Easy

6 tbsp olive oil

1 garlic clove, peeled and crushed

2 tsp Dijon mustard

2 tbsp balsamic vinegar

350g (12oz) freshly cooked pasta shapes (see page 53), drained

2 roasted red peppers, peeled, seeded and sliced

3 tbsp freshly chopped herbs, such as parsley, thyme or basil (if you like)

salt and ground black pepper

1. Mix the oil with the garlic, mustard and vinegar in a small bowl. Stir into the cooked pasta and leave to cool.

2. Season with salt and pepper, add the sliced peppers and serve sprinkled with the herbs, if you like.

STAR QUALITIES

Healthy choice

Handy for packed lunches

Cheap eat

Simple Bean Salad

Serves 6 • Preparation Time 5 minutes, plus 10–15 minutes marinating • Cooking Time 5 minutes • Per Serving 208 calories, 10g fat (of which 2g saturates), 21g carbohydrate, 1.2g salt • Easy

2 tbsp olive oil, plus extra to drizzle

2 garlic cloves, peeled and sliced

2 x 400g cans flageolet beans, drained and rinsed

2 tbsp pesto (see Top Tip, page 90)

lemon juice to taste

a small handful of freash basil leaves (if you like)

salt and ground black pepper

1. Put the oil into a small pan and fry the garlic until golden. Stir in the flageolet beans, then take off the heat and leave to marinate in the oil for 10–15 minutes.

2. When ready to serve, drizzle a little oil over the beans until generously coated. Add the pesto and lemon juice to taste and season with salt and pepper, then stir in the basil leaves, if you like.

SWAP

Instead of flageolet beans, use cannellini, haricot or borlotti beans.

STAR QUALITIES

Ready in under 30 minutes
Healthy choice
Handy for packed lunches

Bean & Chorizo Salad

Serves 4 • Preparation Time 15 minutes • Per Serving 295 calories, 19g fat (of which 4g saturates), 20g carbohydrate, 1.9g salt • Easy

400g can borlotti beans, drained and rinsed
4 large celery sticks, finely sliced
75g (3oz) chorizo sausage, diced
2 shallots, peeled and finely chopped
2 tbsp freshly chopped flat-leafed parsley
grated zest of ½ lemon (see Top Tip, page 85) plus 1 tbsp lemon juice
4 tbsp extra virgin olive oil
salt and ground black pepper

1. Put the borlotti beans into a large bowl and add the celery, chorizo, shallots and parsley.

2. To make the dressing, whisk together the lemon zest, lemon juice and oil in a small bowl. Season with salt and pepper and whisk again to combine.

3. Pour the dressing over the bean mixture, toss together and serve.

SWAP
Instead of shallots use 1 small onion. Use mixed beans or flageolet beans instead of borlotti beans.

MONEYSAVER TIP
Use the remaining celery for: Braised Meat (see page 38) or Easy Tuna Salad (see page 106).

STAR QUALITIES
Ready in under 30 minutes
Healthy choice
Cheap eat

Bacon & Egg Salad

Serves 4 • Preparation Time 10 minutes • Cooking Time 10 minutes • Per Serving 360 calories, 27g fat (of which 8g saturates), 9g carbohydrate, 3.1g salt • Easy

4 medium eggs
250g (9oz) smoked bacon rashers, rinds removed
150g (5oz) cherry tomatoes
2 thick slices bread, with crusts removed
2 tbsp mayonnaise
juice of ½ lemon
25g (1oz) Parmesan, freshly grated
2 Little Gem lettuces
ground black pepper

1. Heat a pan of water until simmering, add the eggs and boil for 6 minutes. Cool completely under cold water, peel and set aside.

2. Meanwhile, heat a frying pan, then fry the bacon for 5 minutes until crisp. Remove from the pan, chop into large pieces and leave to cool.

3. Add the tomatoes and bread to the pan and fry for 2–3 minutes until the bread is crisp and the tomatoes are starting to char.

Remove from the heat, chop the bread into bite-size pieces and put to one side.

4. To make the dressing, put the mayonnaise into a bowl and squeeze in the lemon juice. Add the Parmesan, mix, then season with pepper.

5. Separate the lettuce leaves and put into a large bowl. Add the bacon, tomatoes and bread, toss lightly, then divide among four plates. Cut the eggs in half and add one egg to each plate. Drizzle the dressing over.

STAR QUALITIES
Ready in under 30 minutes
Quick and easy
Cheap eat

Easy Chicken Salad

Serves 1 • Preparation Time 10 minutes • Per Serving 323 calories, 18g fat (of which 5g saturates), 17g carbohydrate, 0.9g salt • Easy

100g (3½oz) shredded cooked chicken, skin discarded (see Moneysaver Tips)
1 carrot, chopped
1 celery stick, chopped
¼ cucumber, chopped
handful of ripe cherry tomatoes, chopped
1 tbsp hummus
¼ lemon to serve

1. Put the chicken into a shallow bowl. Add the carrot, celery, cucumber and cherry tomatoes.

2. Top with the hummus and serve with lemon for squeezing over the salad.

MONEYSAVER TIPS
Use leftover chicken from a roast for this recipe, see page 33
Use the remaining cucumber for: Veggie Pitta (see page 91) or Easy Tuna Salad (see page 106).

TRY SOMETHING DIFFERENT
Add a few pumpkin seeds or sunflower seeds, or a handful of sprouted seeds such as alfalfa, or chopped watercress.
For extra bite, add a little finely chopped red chilli; for extra sweetness, add some strips of red pepper; for extra flavour, add some chopped coriander or torn basil leaves.

STAR QUALITIES
Ready in under 30 minutes
Quick and easy
Healthy choice

BURGERS, SAUSAGES & KEBABS

Speedy Burgers

Makes 4 • Preparation Time 5 minutes • Cooking Time 12–24 minutes • Per Serving 353 calories, 26g fat (of which 11g saturates), 1g carbohydrate, 0.9g salt • Easy

600g (1lb 5oz) minced beef
¼ onion, peeled and grated
1 tsp Worcestershire sauce
1–2 tsp vegetable oil
salt and ground black pepper

1. Mix the mince with the onion and Worcestershire sauce and season well with salt and pepper. Shape into four rounds.

2. Heat the oil in a frying pan and cook the burgers, two at a time if necessary, for 5–6 minutes on each side.

STAR QUALITIES
Ready in under 30 minutes
Quick and easy
Five ingredients or fewer
Comfort food

Chicken Burgers

Serves 2 • Preparation Time 30 minutes, plus 30 minutes chilling • Cooking Time 12 minutes • Per Serving 205 calories, 4g fat (of which 1g saturates), 12g carbohydrate, 0.4g salt • Easy

25g (1oz) fresh bread
225g (8oz) minced chicken
2 shallots, peeled and finely chopped (see Moneysaver Tip)
1 tbsp freshly chopped tarragon
1 large egg yolk
oil to grease
salt and ground black pepper
burger buns, mayonnaise or Greek yogurt, salad leaves and tomato salad to serve

1. If you have one, whiz the bread in a food processor to make fresh breadcrumbs. Otherwise, cut it into strips with a bread knife, then cut the bread up into crumbs, or use a grater (but watch your fingers).

2. Put the chicken into a bowl with the shallots, tarragon, breadcrumbs and egg yolk. Mix well, then beat in about 75ml (3fl oz) cold water and season with salt and pepper.

3. Lightly oil a foil-lined baking sheet. Divide the chicken mixture into four portions and place on the foil. Using the back of a wet spoon, flatten each portion to a thickness of 2.5cm (1in). Cover and chill for 30 minutes.

4. Preheat the barbecue or grill. Cook the burgers for 5–6 minutes on each side until cooked through, then serve in a toasted burger bun with a dollop of mayonnaise or Greek yogurt, a few salad leaves and tomato salad.

MONEYSAVER TIP
Instead of shallots, use 1 onion.

TRY SOMETHING DIFFERENT
Pork and Apricot Burgers
Replace the chicken with minced pork, use chopped sage instead of tarragon and add 100g (3½oz) chopped ready-to-eat dried apricots to the mixture before shaping.

STAR QUALITIES
Healthy choice
Comfort food
Share with friends
Make in advance, cook later

Sausages: 3 Cooking Methods

Serves 4, makes 450ml (¾ pint) • Preparation Time 5 minutes • Cooking Time 30 minutes • Per Serving 64 calories, 3g fat (of which trace saturates), 9g carbohydrate, 0.6g salt • Easy

1 tbsp oil

1 red onion, peeled and finely sliced

1 tbsp plain flour

½ tsp tomato purée

1 beef stock cube

450ml (¾ pint) boiling water

2 bay leaves

Sausages come in loads of flavours and are easy to cook.

Fried sausages

Melt a little fat in a frying pan, add the sausages and fry for 15–20 minutes, keeping the heat low to prevent them burning and turning them once or twice to brown them evenly.

Grilled sausages

Heat the grill to hot, put the sausages on the grill rack in the grill pan and cook until one side is lightly browned, then turn them; continue cooking and turning them frequently for 15–20 minutes, until the sausages are well browned.

Baked sausages

Heat the oven to 200°C (180°C fan oven) mark 6. Put the sausages into a greased baking tin and cook in the centre of the oven for 30 minutes.

Quick Onion Gravy for Sausages

1. Heat the oil in a pan. Add the onion and fry for 10 minutes or until soft. Stir in the flour and tomato purée and cook for 1 minute.

2. Crumble in the beef stock cube, water and bay leaves. Bring to the boil, then reduce the heat and simmer for 15 minutes. Season to taste with salt and pepper, remove the bay leaves and serve with sausages and mash.

Spiced Pork with Lemon Pasta

Serves 6 • Preparation Time 10 minutes • Cooking Time 12 minutes • Per Serving 733 calories, 44g fat (of which 28g saturates), 71g carbohydrate, 1.8g salt • Easy

8 thick pork sausages
500g (1lb 2oz) dried pasta shells or other shapes
100ml (3½fl oz) dry white wine
grated zest of 1 lemon
juice of ½ lemon
large pinch of dried chilli flakes
300ml (½ pint) half-fat crème fraîche
2 tbsp freshly chopped flat-leafed parsley
25g (1oz) Parmesan, freshly grated
salt and ground black pepper

1. Remove the skin from the sausages and pinch the meat into small pieces. Heat a non-stick frying pan over a medium heat. When hot, add the sausagemeat and cook for 5 minutes, stirring occasionally, until cooked through and browned.

2. Meanwhile, cook the pasta according to the instructions on the pack until al dente.

3. Add the wine to the sausagemeat, bring to a-= boil and let bubble, stirring, for 2–3 minutes until the liquid has reduced right down. Add the lemon zest and juice, chilli flakes and crème fraîche. Season well with salt and pepper. Continue to cook for 3–4 minutes until reduced and thickened slightly.

4. Drain the pasta and return to the pan. Stir the parsley into the sauce and toss with the pasta. Serve immediately, with Parmesan.

Spicy Sausages

Serves 4 • Preparation Time 5 minutes • Cooking Time 30 minutes • Per Serving 414 calories, 26g fat (of which 10g saturates), 34g carbohydrate, 4.1g salt • Easy

4 tbsp hot chilli sauce
4 tbsp clear honey
450g (1lb) coarse pork sausages
  (about 8)

1. Preheat the oven to 200°C (180°C fan oven) mark 6. Mix together the hot chilli sauce and honey.

2. Put the sausages into a small roasting tin and cook in the oven for about 10 minutes. Add the sauce and stir to coat the sausages on all sides. Cook for a further

20 minutes or until golden brown and cooked through. Serve with mashed potatoes (see page 51) or stir-fried vegetables (see page 60).

STAR QUALITIES
Five ingredients or fewer
Cheap eat
Comfort food
Share with friends

Sausages & Fried Potatoes

Serves 4 • Preparation Time 15 minutes • Cooking Time 35 minutes • Per Serving 622 calories, 39g fat (of which 17g saturates), 51g carbohydrate, 3.3g salt • Easy

**700g (1½lb) medium potatoes,
    unpeeled**
50g (2oz) butter
1 small onion, peeled and chopped
450g (1lb) pork sausages
**2 red onions, peeled and cut into
    rings**
sunflower oil to brush
450g (1lb) small tomatoes
salt

1. Put the potatoes into a pan of lightly salted water, bring to the boil and par-boil for 10 minutes. Drain, then cut into 2.5cm (1in) cubes.

2. Heat the butter in a large frying pan. Add the chopped onion and fry for 1 minute. Add the potatoes and fry over a medium heat for 25 minutes or until crisp and brown, turning frequently. Meanwhile, preheat the grill to medium-high.

3. Grill the sausages for about 20 minutes, turning from time to time, until browned and cooked through to the centre. Halfway through cooking, brush the onion rings with oil and add to the grill pan with the tomatoes. Grill until softened and lightly caramelised.

4. Serve the sausages on top of the potatoes, with the onion rings and tomatoes.

STAR QUALITIES
Comfort food
Share with friends

Sausages with Roasted Potato & Onion Wedges

Serves 4 • Preparation Time 10 minutes • Cooking Time 1 hour 20 minutes • Per Serving 569 calories, 33g fat (of which 10g saturates), 53g carbohydrate, 2.8g salt • Easy

900g (2lb) large potatoes, peeled and cut into wedges
4 tbsp olive oil
3–4 fresh rosemary sprigs (if you like)
2 red onions, peeled and each cut into eight wedges
8 sausages
salt and ground black pepper

1. Preheat the oven to 220°C (200°C fan oven) mark 7. Put the potatoes into a roasting tin – they should sit in one layer. Drizzle the oil over them and season with salt and pepper. Toss well to coat the potatoes in oil, then put the rosemary on top, if you like, and roast in the oven for 20 minutes.

2. Remove the roasting tin from the oven (use oven gloves) and add the onion wedges. Toss again to coat the onions and potatoes. Put the sausages in between the potatoes and onions. Return the tin to the oven for 50 minutes to 1 hour.

TIMESAVER TIP
Set the alarm on your mobile phone, or use a timer, and let the oven do the work while you get on with other things.

SWAP
Instead of red onions, use white.

STAR QUALITIES
Cheap eat
Share with friends
Great for parties

Potato & Sausage Skewers

Serves 6 • Preparation Time 15 minutes plus soaking • Cooking Time 18 minutes • Per Serving 789 calories, 52g fat (of which 17g saturates), 58g carbohydrate, 4g salt • Easy

36 even-sized new potatoes, scrubbed
6 tbsp olive oil, plus extra to brush
12 thick sausages
2 tbsp freshly chopped mint
50g (2oz) freshly grated Parmesan
salt and ground black pepper
rocket to serve (if you like)

1. Preheat the grill or barbecue. Soak twelve wooden skewers in water for 20 minutes. Boil the potatoes in lightly salted water for about 10 minutes or until almost tender. Drain well and toss with the oil, then season with salt and pepper.

2. Cut each sausage into three and thread on to the skewers alternately with the potatoes. Brush with oil and grill or barbecue for about 8 minutes, turning from time to time, until the sausages are cooked through and the potatoes begin to char.

3. Meanwhile, put the mint into a bowl, add the Parmesan and stir together until well mixed.

4. When the sausages are cooked, remove from the grill or barbecue and, while still hot, sprinkle with the mint and Parmesan mixture. Serve with rocket, if you like.

STAR QUALITIES
Cheap eat
Comfort food
Share with friends
Great for parties

Mediterranean Kebabs

Serves 4 • Preparation Time 15 minutes, plus soaking • Cooking Time 8–10 minutes • Per Serving 164 calories, 13g fat (of which 5g saturates), 7g carbohydrate, 1.1g salt • Easy

1 large courgette, trimmed and cut into chunks

1 red pepper, seeded and cut into chunks (see page 44)

12 cherry tomatoes

125g (4oz) halloumi cheese, cubed

100g (3½oz) natural yogurt

1 tsp ground cumin

2 tbsp olive oil

squeeze of lemon

1 lemon, cut into eight wedges

couscous tossed with freshly chopped flat-leafed parsley to serve (see **Top Tip**, page 181)

1. Preheat the barbecue or grill. Soak eight wooden skewers in water for 20 minutes. Put the courgette into a large bowl with the red pepper, cherry tomatoes and halloumi cheese. Add the yogurt, cumin, olive oil and a squeeze of lemon and mix.

2. Push a lemon wedge on to each skewer, then divide the vegetables and cheese among the skewers. Grill the kebabs, turning them regularly, for 8–10 minutes until the vegetables are tender and the halloumi is nicely charred. Serve with couscous.

STAR QUALITIES
Ready in under 30 minutes
Cheap eat
Share with friends
Great for parties

Moroccan Spiced Chicken Kebabs

Serves 4 • Preparation Time 10 minutes, plus minimum 20 minutes marinating • Cooking Time 10–12 minutes • Per Serving 189 calories, 5g fat (of which 1g saturates), 1g carbohydrate, 0.2g salt • Easy

2 tbsp olive oil

15g (½oz) flat-leafed parsley

1 garlic clove, peeled

½ tsp paprika

1 tsp ground cumin

grated zest and juice of 1 lemon (see Top Tip, page 85)

4 skinless chicken thighs, cut into bite-size chunks

couscous salad (see Top Tip, page 181) and lime wedges to serve

1. Put the oil, parsley, garlic, paprika, cumin, lemon zest and juice into a bowl and use a stick blender to whiz to a paste.

2. Put the chicken into a shallow dish and add the spice paste, then rub in and leave to marinate for at least 20 minutes.

3. Preheat the barbecue or grill. Soak four wooden skewers in water for 20 minutes.

4. Thread the marinated chicken on to the skewers and grill for 10–12 minutes, turning every now and then, until cooked through. Serve with couscous salad and lime wedges.

EQUIPMENT ALERT
You'll need a stick blender for this one.

STAR QUALITIES
Healthy choice
Cheap eat
Comfort food
Share with friends

Spiced Tikka Kebabs

Serves 4 • Preparation Time 10 minutes • Cooking Time 20 minutes • Per Serving 150 calories, 5g fat (of which 1g saturates), 4g carbohydrate, 0.3g salt • Easy

2 tbsp tikka paste
150g (5oz) natural yogurt
juice of ½ lime (see Moneysaver Tips)
4 spring onions, chopped
350g (12oz) boneless, skinless chicken thighs, cut into bite-size pieces
lime wedges to serve (if you like)

1. Preheat the grill. Put the tikka paste, yogurt, lime juice and chopped spring onions into a large bowl. Add the chicken and toss well. Thread the chicken on to skewers.

2. Grill for 8–10 minutes on each side until cooked through, turning and basting with the paste. Serve with lime wedges to squeeze over the kebabs, if you like.

MONEYSAVER TIPS

Instead of lime, use a lemon. Instead of boneless thighs, buy thighs on the bone and cut the meat off.

TOP TIP

Serve with Rocket Salad
Put 75g (3oz) rocket in a large bowl. Add ¼ chopped avocado, a handful of halved cherry tomatoes, ½ chopped cucumber and the juice of 1 lime or lemon. Season with salt and pepper and mix together.

STAR QUALITIES

Ready in under 30 minutes
Healthy choice
Comfort food
Share with friends

Spiced Lamb in Pitta

Serves 4 • Preparation Time 20 minutes, plus 30 minutes chilling • Cooking Time 8–10 minutes
Per Serving 550 calories, 20g fat (of which 9g saturates), 60g carbohydrate, 1.3g salt • Easy

**1 small green pepper, seeded and
   chopped (see page 44)**
½ small onion, peeled and chopped
3 garlic cloves, peeled
2 tsp ground cumin
3 tbsp olive oil
1 tbsp freshly chopped mint
550g (1¼lb) lean minced lamb
**450g (1lb) very ripe tomatoes,
   chopped**
**2 tbsp freshly chopped flat-leafed
   parsley**
4 large pitta breads
salt and ground black pepper
mint sprigs to garnish (if you like)
Greek yogurt to serve

1. Put the chopped pepper and onion into a bowl with the garlic, cumin and oil and use a stick blender to form a coarse paste. Add the chopped mint. Mix together the paste and the minced lamb, season with salt and pepper and shape into 16 patties. Chill for 30 minutes or overnight.

2. Put the tomatoes into a bowl, stir in the parsley and season with salt and pepper.

3. Preheat the barbecue, griddle or grill. Cook the lamb patties for 4–5 minutes on each side. Warm the pitta breads, wrap into a cone and secure with a cocktail stick. Fill each with four lamb patties and spoon on a drizzle of yogurt. Serve with the tomatoes and garnish with mint sprigs, if you like.

EQUIPMENT ALERT
*You'll need a stick blender for
this one.*

FREEZING TIP
*Complete the recipe to the end
of step 1, place the patties on
a tray to freeze, then wrap, label
and freeze for up to one month.*
To use *Thaw at cool room
temperature for four hours.
Complete the recipe.*

COMFORT FOOD
*Share with friends
Great for parties
Make in advance, cook later*

PASTA & GNOCCHI

Quick Tomato Sauce

Serves 4 • Preparation Time 10 minutes • Cooking Time 35 minutes • Per Serving 46 calories, 3g fat (of which trace saturates), 4g carbohydrate, 0.7g salt • Easy

1 tbsp olive oil
1 small onion, peeled and finely chopped
1 garlic clove, peeled and chopped
400g can plum tomatoes
salt and ground black pepper

1. Heat the oil in a medium pan for 30 seconds, then add the onion and fry gently for 15 minutes, stirring regularly, or until the onion is softened and translucent but not browned.

2. Add the garlic and continue to cook gently for 1 minute. Stir in the tomatoes. Fill the empty tomato can up to about half with cold water and give it a swirl to catch any tomato juice. Pour into the pan, then season with salt and pepper. Turn up the heat to medium and simmer the sauce for about 15 minutes or until it's thickened slightly.

TOP TIP

Spaghetti with Tomato Sauce

While the sauce is simmering, cook 500g (1lb 2oz) spaghetti in a large pan of boiling water (see Cooking Pasta on page 53). Drain well, reserving about a cup of the cooking water. Return the pasta to the pan, add the tomato sauce and mix well. Add a splash or two of the cooking water to loosen the pasta and sauce. Grate some Cheddar cheese over the pasta and season generously with salt and black pepper. Serves 4.

STAR QUALITIES

Healthy choice
Five ingredients or fewer
Cheap eat
Comfort food

Five Great Pasta Sauce Recipes to make from Quick Tomato Sauce

With tuna

Drain an 80g can of tuna in oil or brine (you can use some of the oil to cook the onion in step 1 of the sauce opposite). When the tomato sauce has thickened and finished simmering, stir in the drained tuna and cook for 2–3 minutes to warm through. Toss with pasta. Serves 4.

With bacon

Chop 2 rindless streaky bacon rashers and add to the pan with the onion at step 1 opposite. Cook for 10–15 minutes until the bacon is browned, then add the garlic and tomatoes and complete the recipe as above. Serves 4.

With red pepper and olives

Add 1 seeded and sliced red pepper (see page 44) to the pan when frying the onion at step 1 opposite, then complete the recipe as opposite. When the tomato sauce has finished simmering, add 6 pitted, chopped olives and cook for 1–2 minutes to heat through. Serves 4.

With chilli

Fry ½ finely chopped and seeded red chilli (see page 44) with the onion (or use ½ tsp dried chilli flakes), then complete the recipe as opposite. Serves 4.

With basil

After cooking the sauce, stir in a handful of freshly chopped basil. Serves 4.

Simple Meat Sauce

Serves 4 • Preparation Time 15 minutes • Cooking time 40 minutes • Per Serving 310 calories, 21g fat
(of which 8g saturates), 6g carbohydrate, 2.5g salt • Easy

1 tbsp olive oil
1 onion, peeled and finely chopped
2 garlic cloves, peeled and crushed
450g (1lb) minced beef
300ml (½ pint) beef stock
  (see Top Tips)
2 tbsp tomato purée
400g can chopped tomatoes
2 tbsp Worcestershire sauce
125g (4oz) button mushrooms,
  sliced
salt and ground black pepper

1. Heat the oil in a large pan, add the onion and fry over a medium heat for 15 minutes or until softened and golden. Add the garlic and cook for 1 minute.

2. Add the mince and, as it browns, use a wooden spoon to break up the pieces. Stir the stock and tomato purée into the browned mince, cover the pan with a lid and bring to the boil. Add the tomatoes, Worcestershire sauce and mushrooms and season well with salt and pepper. Bring back to the boil, then reduce the heat and simmer, stirring occasionally, for 20 minutes.

MONEYSAVER TIP

Replace half the quantity of mince with 200g (7oz) red lentils and add them after browning the mince. There's no need to soak them, so just stir them in and complete the recipe.

TOP TIPS

You can use 1 beef stock cube dissolved in 300ml (½ pint) boiling water.

Spaghetti Bolognese

About 15 minutes before the sauce has finished cooking, cook 500g (1lb 2oz) spaghetti in a large pan of boiling water (see Cooking Pasta, page 53). Drain well, reserving about a cup of the cooking water. Return the pasta to the pan, add the meat sauce and mix well. Add a splash or two of the cooking water to loosen the pasta and sauce. Grate some Cheddar cheese over the pasta and serve.

Chilli Bolognese

To spice up the basic meat sauce, add ½ large red seeded chilli (see page 44) to the onion when frying in step 1.

STAR QUALITIES

Cheap eat
Comfort food
Share with friends

Six Quick Pasta Sauces

Lemon & Parmesan

Cook pasta shells in a large pan of lightly salted boiling water for the time stated on the pack. Add 125g (4oz) frozen peas to the pasta water for the last 5 minutes of the cooking time. Drain the pasta and peas, put back into the pan and add the grated zest and juice of ½ lemon and 75g (3oz) freshly grated Parmesan. Season with ground black pepper, toss and serve immediately.

Tomato, Prawn & Garlic

Put 350g (12oz) cooked peeled prawns into a bowl with 4 tbsp tomato purée and stir well. Heat 1 tbsp olive oil and 15g (½oz) butter in a frying pan and gently cook 3 peeled and sliced garlic cloves until golden. Add 4 large chopped tomatoes and 125ml (4fl oz) dry white wine. Leave the sauce to bubble for about 5 minutes, then stir in the prawns and some freshly chopped parsley.

Courgette & Anchovy

Heat the oil from a 50g can anchovies in a frying pan. Add 1 peeled and crushed garlic clove and a pinch of dried chilli and cook for 1 minute. Add 400ml (14fl oz) passata sauce (puréed and sieved tomatoes, available in jars), 2 diced courgettes and the anchovies. Bring to the boil, then reduce the heat and simmer for about 10 minutes, stirring well, until the anchovies have melted.

Broccoli & Thyme

Put 900g (2lb) trimmed broccoli into a pan with 150ml (¼ pint) hot vegetable stock. Bring to the boil, then cover and simmer for 3–4 minutes until tender – the stock should have evaporated. Add 2 peeled and crushed garlic cloves and 2 tbsp olive oil and cook for 1–2 minutes to soften the garlic. Add 250g carton mascarpone, 2 tbsp freshly chopped thyme and 100g (3½oz) freshly grated cheese and mix together. Season with salt and ground black pepper.

Quick & Easy Carbonara

Fry 150g (5oz) chopped smoked bacon rashers in 1 tbsp oil for 4–5 minutes. Add to drained, cooked pasta, such as tagliatelle, and keep hot. Put 2 large egg yolks into a bowl, add 150ml (¼ pint) double cream and whisk together. Add to the pasta with 50g (2oz) freshly grated Parmesan and 2 tbsp freshly chopped parsley.

Luxury Mushroom & Cream

Heat 1 tbsp olive oil in a large pan and fry 1 peeled and finely chopped onion for 7–10 minutes until soft. Add 300g (11oz) sliced mushrooms and cook for 3–4 minutes. Pour in 125ml (4fl oz) dry white wine and bubble for 1 minute, then stir in 500ml (18fl oz) low-fat crème fraîche. Heat until bubbling, then stir in 2 tbsp freshly chopped tarragon. Season to taste with salt and ground black pepper.

Simple Chilli Pasta

Serves 4 • Preparation Time 5 minutes • Cooking Time about 10 minutes • Per Serving 369 calories, 6g fat (of which 1g saturates), 71g carbohydrate, 0.9g salt • Easy

350g (12oz) spaghetti
1 tbsp olive oil
2 garlic cloves, peeled and crushed
1 red chilli, seeded and chopped
  (see page 44)
2 x 400g cans chopped tomatoes
  with herbs
20g packet fresh basil
50g (2oz) pitted black olives

1. Cook the spaghetti in a large pan of lightly salted boiling water according to the pack instructions. Drain and return to the pan.

2. Meanwhile, heat the oil in another pan. Tip the garlic and chilli into the pan and fry for 2 minutes, stirring all the time. Add the tomatoes and cook for 5 minutes or until bubbling.

3. Tear the basil leaves and add them to the tomatoes with the olives. Tip the mixture into the drained spaghetti, stir well and serve.

STAR QUALITIES
Ready in under 30 minutes
Quick and easy
Healthy choice
Cheap eat

Bacon, Chilli & Herb Pasta

Serves 4 • Preparation Time 5 minutes • Cooking Time 10 minutes • Per Serving 545 calories, 21g fat
(of which 10g saturates), 76g carbohydrate, 1.4g salt • Easy

400g (14oz) dried fusilli pasta
150g (5oz) smoked streaky bacon, chopped
50g (2oz) butter
1 tbsp freshly chopped parsley or sage
½ red chilli, seeded and finely chopped (see page 44)
salt and ground black pepper

1. Cook the pasta in a large pan of lightly salted boiling water according to the pack instructions.

2. Heat a large pan and fry the bacon for 3 minutes.

3. Add the butter, parsley or sage and chilli, and cook for 30 seconds. Season with pepper.

4. Drain the pasta and tip into a bowl, then stir the sauce into the pasta and serve.

STAR QUALITIES
Ready in under 30 minutes
Five ingredients or fewer
Cheap eat
Comfort food

Fusilli with Chilli & Tomatoes

Serves 4 • Preparation Time 10 minutes • Cooking Time 10–15 minutes • Per Serving 479 calories, 17g fat
(of which 4g saturates), 69g carbohydrate, 0.4g salt • Easy

**350g (12oz) fusilli or other short
    dried pasta**
4 tbsp olive oil
**1 large red chilli, seeded and finely
    chopped (see page 44)**
1 garlic clove, peeled and crushed
500g (1lb 2oz) cherry tomatoes
2 tbsp freshly chopped basil
**50g (2oz) Parmesan, shaved
    (see Top Tip)**
salt and ground black pepper

1. Cook the pasta in a large pan
of lightly salted boiling water
according to the pack instructions.
Drain.

2. Meanwhile, heat the oil in a
large frying pan over a high heat.
Add the chilli and garlic and cook
for 30 seconds. Add the tomatoes,
season with salt and pepper and
cook over a high heat for 3 minutes
or until the skins begin to split.

3. Add the basil and drained
pasta and toss together. Transfer
to a dish, sprinkle the Parmesan
shavings over the top and
serve immediately.

TOP TIP
*Make Parmesan shavings with a
vegetable peeler. Hold the piece
of cheese in one hand and pare off
wafer-thin strips of cheese using
the peeler.*

STAR QUALITIES
*Ready in under 30 minutes
Quick and easy
Healthy choice
Cheap eat*

Spicy Tomato Pasta

Serves 4 • Preparation Time 5 minutes • Cooking Time 15 minutes • Per Serving 343 calories, 7g fat (of which 1g saturates), 61g carbohydrate, 2g salt • Easy

300g (11oz) chunky pasta shapes
50g jar anchovies in oil with garlic and herbs
6 tomatoes, chopped
75g (3oz) pitted black olives, chopped
1 lemon, cut into wedges (if you like)

1. Cook the pasta in a large pan of lightly salted boiling water according to the pack instructions.

2. Drain the oil from the anchovies into a bowl and put 1 tbsp into a pan. Heat gently for 1 minute. Use the remaining oil for another recipe (see Top Tip).

3. Add the anchovies to the hot oil and cook for 1 minute. Add the tomatoes and simmer for 10 minutes. Stir in the olives and cook for 1–2 minutes more.

4. Drain the pasta, tip back into the pan and add the sauce. Toss together and serve with lemon wedges, if you like.

TOP TIP
Keep the oil from the anchovies in the fridge for up to three days and use when frying onions to give them added flavour.

QUICK AND EASY
Healthy and sustaining
Five ingredients or fewer
Cheap eat

Roast Tomato Pasta

Serves 4 • Preparation Time 5 minutes • Cooking Time 15 minutes • Per Serving 507 calories, 16g fat (of which 2g saturates), 80g carbohydrate, trace salt • Easy

400g (14oz) dried rigatoni pasta
700g (1½lb) cherry tomatoes
olive oil to drizzle
50g (2oz) pinenuts
a large handful of fresh basil
   leaves, torn
salt and ground black pepper
freshly grated Parmesan to serve

1. Preheat the oven to 240°C (220°C fan oven) mark 9. Cook the pasta in a large pan of lightly salted boiling water according to the pack instructions.

2. Meanwhile, cut half the tomatoes in two and arrange them in a large roasting tin, cut side up. Add the remaining whole tomatoes and drizzle all with oil. Season with salt and pepper. Put the pinenuts on to a separate roasting tray and roast both in the oven for 15 minutes or until the tomatoes are softened and lightly caramelised. Watch carefully to make sure the pinenuts don't scorch and remove from the oven earlier if necessary.

3. Drain the pasta well and add to the roasting tin when the tomatoes are done. Scatter the basil and pinenuts over, then stir thoroughly to coat the pasta in the juices. Adjust the seasoning and stir in a little more oil, if you like. Sprinkle with Parmesan and serve.

STAR QUALITIES
Ready in under 30 minutes
Quick and easy
Healthy choice

Ham & Mushroom Pasta

Serves 4 • Preparation Time 5 minutes • Cooking Time 15 minutes • Per Serving 415 calories, 10g fat (of which 4g saturates), 67g carbohydrate, 1g salt • Easy

350g (12oz) penne pasta
1 tbsp olive oil
2 shallots, sliced
200g (7oz) small button mushrooms
3 tbsp crème fraîche (see Moneysaver Tip)
125g (4oz) cooked ham, roughly chopped (smoked is nice)
2 tbsp freshly chopped flat-leafed parsley
salt and ground black pepper

1. Cook the pasta in a large pan of lightly salted boiling water according to the pack instructions.

2. Meanwhile, heat the oil in a pan. Add the shallots and fry gently for 3 minutes or until starting to soften. Add the mushrooms and fry for 5–6 minutes.

3. Drain the pasta, put back into the pan and add the shallots and mushrooms. Stir in the crème fraîche, ham and parsley. Toss everything together, season with salt and pepper and heat through to serve.

MONEYSAVER TIP
Instead of crème fraîche use cream or Greek yogurt.

STAR QUALITIES
Ready in under 30 minutes
Quick and easy
Cheap eat
Comfort food

Pasta with Pesto & Beans

Serves 4 • Preparation Time 5 minutes • Cooking Time 15 minutes • Per Serving 738 calories, 38g fat (of which 10g saturates), 74g carbohydrate, 1g salt • Easy

350g (12oz) dried pasta shapes
175g (6oz) fine green beans,
  roughly chopped
175g (6oz) small potatoes, thickly
  sliced
250g (9oz) pesto (see Top Tip,
  page 90)
Parmesan shavings to serve
  (see Top Tip, page 138)

1. Bring a large pan of lightly salted water to the boil. Add the pasta, bring back to the boil and cook for 5 minutes.

2. Add the beans and potatoes to the pan and boil for a further 7–8 minutes until the potatoes are just tender.

3. Drain the pasta, beans and potatoes in a colander, then tip everything back into the pan and stir in the pesto. Serve scattered with Parmesan shavings.

MONEYSAVER TIP
Use leftover cooked pasta, beans or potatoes: tip the pasta into a pan of boiling water and bring back to the boil for 30 seconds. Bring the beans or potatoes to room temperature, but there's no need to reboil them.

Fast Macaroni Cheese

Serves 4 • Preparation Time 5 minutes • Cooking Time 15 minutes • Per Serving 215 calories, 11g fat (of which 6g saturates), 21g carbohydrate, 1.1g salt • Easy

300g (11oz) macaroni
drizzle of oil
1 quantity cheese sauce
   (see page 23)
freshly chopped flat-leafed parsley
   (if you like)
extra grated cheese to sprinkle
salt and ground black pepper

1. Preheat the grill to high. Cook the macaroni in a large pan of lightly salted boiling water according to the pack instructions. Drain well, then put into a 1.1 litre (2 pint) ovenproof dish. Add a drizzle of oil, season well and stir to mix. Stir in the cheese sauce, and the parsley, if you like.

2. Sprinkle the grated cheese over the macaroni. Put under the grill for 5 minutes or until golden brown on top and bubbling. Serve immediately.

Chicken, Bacon & Leek Pasta Bake

Serves 4 • Preparation Time 10 minutes • Cooking Time about 20 minutes • Per Serving 650 calories, 24g fat (of which 6g saturates), 68g carbohydrate, 2.2g salt • Easy

1 tbsp olive oil

100g (3½oz) chopped streaky bacon rashers

450g (1lb) boneless, skinless chicken thighs, chopped

3 medium leeks, trimmed and chopped

300g (11oz) macaroni or other pasta shapes

350g carton ready-made cheese sauce

2 tsp Dijon mustard

2 tbsp freshly chopped flat-leafed parsley

25g (1oz) freshly grated Parmesan

1. Heat the oil in a large frying pan. Add the bacon and chicken and cook for 7–8 minutes. Add the leeks and continue cooking for 4–5 minutes.

2. Meanwhile, cook the pasta in a large pan of lightly salted boiling water according to the pack instructions. Drain well.

3. Preheat the grill. Add the cheese sauce to the pasta with the mustard, chicken mixture and parsley. Mix well, then tip into a 2.1 litre (3¾ pint) ovenproof dish and sprinkle with Parmesan. Grill for 4–5 minutes until golden.

MONEYSAVER TIPS

Instead of boneless chicken thighs, buy thighs on the bone and cut the meat off.

Make home-made cheese sauce (see page 23).

Very Easy Four Cheese Gnocchi

Serves 4 • Preparation Time 2 minutes • Cooking Time 20 minutes • Per Serving 580 calories, 24g fat (of which 12g saturates), 75g carbohydrate, 0.5g salt • Easy

2 tsp salt
2 x 350g packs fresh gnocchi
500g tub fresh four-cheese sauce
2 x 240g packs sunblush tomatoes
4 tbsp freashly torn basil leaves
2 tbsp freshly grated Parmesan
25g (1oz) butter, chopped
salt and ground black pepper

1. Bring two large pans of water to the boil, add 1 tsp salt and 1 pack gnocchi to each and cook for the time stated on the pack or until all the pieces have floated to the surface. Drain well and put back into one pan.

2. Preheat the grill. Pour the cheese sauce and tomatoes over the gnocchi and heat gently, stirring, for 2 minutes. Season, then add the basil and stir again. Put into individual heatproof bowls, sprinkle the Parmesan over and

dot with the butter. Grill for 3–5 minutes until golden and bubbling, then serve.

STAR QUALITIES
Ready in under 30 minutes
Quick and easy
Comfort food
Share with friends

BEANS & LENTILS

Mushroom & Bean Hotpot

Serves 6 • Preparation Time 15 minutes • Cooking Time 30 minutes • Per Serving 244 calories, 8g fat (of which 1g saturates), 35g carbohydrate, 2g salt • Easy

3 tbsp olive oil

700g (1½lb) chestnut mushrooms, roughly chopped

1 large onion, peeled and finely chopped

2 tbsp plain flour

2 tbsp mild curry paste

150ml (¼ pint) hot vegetable stock (see Top Tip)

400g can chopped tomatoes

2 tbsp sun-dried tomato paste (see Moneysaver Tip)

2 x 400g cans mixed beans, drained and rinsed

3 tbsp mango chutney

3 tbsp roughly chopped fresh coriander and mint

1. Heat the oil in a large pan over a low heat and fry the mushrooms and onion until the onion is soft and dark golden. Stir in the flour and curry paste and cook for 1–2 minutes, then add the hot stock, tomatoes, sun-dried tomato paste and beans.

2. Bring to the boil, then simmer gently for 30 minutes or until most of the liquid has reduced. Stir in the chutney and herbs before serving.

MONEYSAVER TIPS
Instead of chestnut mushrooms, use white mushrooms.
Use fresh parsley instead of coriander and mint.
Use tomato purée instead of sun-dried tomato paste.

TOP TIP
You can use ½ vegetable stock cube dissolved in 150ml (¼ pint) boiling water.

STAR QUALITIES
Healthy and sustaining
Cheap eat

Black-eyed Bean Chilli

Serves 4 • Preparation Time 10 minutes • Cooking Time 20 minutes • Per Serving 245 calories, 5g fat (of which 1g saturates), 39g carbohydrate, 1.8g salt • Easy

1 tbsp olive oil
1 onion, peeled and chopped
3 celery sticks, finely chopped
2 x 400g cans black-eyed beans,
    drained and rinsed
2 x 400g cans chopped tomatoes
2 or 3 splashes of Tabasco sauce
3 tbsp freshly chopped coriander
4 warmed tortillas and soured
    cream to serve

1. Heat the oil in a frying pan. Add the onion and celery and cook for 10 minutes or until softened.

2. Add the beans, tomatoes and Tabasco sauce to the pan. Bring to the boil, then reduce the heat and simmer for 10 minutes.

3. Just before serving, stir in the coriander. Spoon the chilli on to the warm tortillas, roll up and serve with soured cream.

MONEYSAVER TIPS
Instead of soured cream, use yogurt.
Use parsley instead of coriander.
Use the remaining celery for:
Braised Meat, page 38
Falafel, Rocket & Soured Cream
Wrap, page 93
Easy Tuna Salad, page 106

STAR QUALITIES
Quick and easy
Healthy and sustaining
Cheap eat
Comfort food

Chickpea Patties

Serves 4 • Preparation Time 20 minutes, plus chilling • Cooking Time about 15 minutes • Per Serving 344 calories, 17g fat (of which 2g saturates), 37g carbohydrate, 1g salt • Easy

2 x 400g cans chickpeas, drained and rinsed
4 garlic cloves, peeled and crushed
1 tsp ground cumin
1 small red onion, peeled and finely chopped
20g pack fresh coriander, chopped
2 tbsp plain flour, plus extra to dust
olive oil for frying
mixed salad and lemon wedges to serve

1. Pat the chickpeas dry with kitchen paper, then mash them with the garlic, cumin, onion and coriander. Stir in the flour.

2. With floured hands, shape the chickpea mixture into 12 small, round patties and chill in the fridge for 20 minutes.

3. Heat a little oil in a non-stick frying pan over a medium heat and fry the patties in batches for about 2 minutes on each side or until heated through and golden. Serve warm with mixed salad and lemon wedges.

STAR QUALITIES
Healthy choice
Cheap eat
Comfort food
Share with friends

Chickpea & Chilli Stir-fry

Serves 4 • Preparation Time 10 minutes • Cooking Time 15–20 minutes • Per Serving 258 calories, 11g fat (of which 1g saturates), 30g carbohydrate, 1g salt • Easy

2 tbsp olive oil

1 tsp ground cumin

1 red onion, peeled and sliced (see Moneysaver Tips)

2 garlic cloves, peeled and finely chopped

1 red chilli, seeded and finely chopped (see page 44)

2 x 400g cans chickpeas, drained and rinsed

400g (14oz) cherry tomatoes

125g (4oz) baby spinach leaves (see Moneysaver Tips)

brown rice or pasta to serve (see pages 55 and 53)

1. Heat the oil in a wok. Add the ground cumin and fry for 1–2 minutes. Add the onion and stir-fry for 5–7 minutes.

2. Add the garlic and chilli and stir-fry for 2 minutes.

3. Add the chickpeas to the wok with the tomatoes. Reduce the heat and simmer until the chickpeas are hot. Add the spinach and stir to wilt. Serve with brown rice or pasta.

MONEYSAVER TIPS

Instead of red onion, use white. Use shredded spinach instead of baby spinach.

Hot Spiced Chickpeas

Serves 4 • Preparation Time 5 minutes • Cooking Time 10–15 minutes • Per Serving 201 calories, 7g fat (of which 1g saturates), 27g carbohydrate, 0.7g salt • Easy

1 tbsp oil
1 onion, peeled and chopped
2 tsp ground turmeric
1 tbsp cumin seeds
450g (1lb) tomatoes, roughly
    chopped
2 x 400g cans chickpeas, drained
    and rinsed
1 tbsp lemon juice
4 tbsp freshly chopped coriander
salt and ground black pepper
fresh coriander leaves to garnish
    (if you like)

1. Heat the oil in a pan. Add the onion and cook for 5–10 minutes until golden brown, stirring constantly.

2. Add the turmeric and cumin seeds and cook, stirring, for 1–2 minutes. Add the tomatoes and chickpeas to the pan together with the lemon juice, coriander and seasoning. Cook for 1–2 minutes, stirring frequently.

3. Garnish with coriander leaves, if you like, and serve with baked potatoes, rice or wholemeal bread.

SWAP
Instead of coriander, use parsley.

STAR QUALITIES
Ready in under 30 minutes
Quick and easy
Healthy and sustaining
Cheap eat

Warm Lentil Salad

Serves 2 • Preparation Time 15 minutes • Cooking Time 10 minutes • Per Serving 300 calories, 10g fat (of which 2g saturates), 33g carbohydrate, trace salt • Easy

2 medium eggs

2 tsp olive oil

2 small leeks, chopped

4 spring onions, chopped

1 red pepper, seeded and chopped (see page 44)

400g can lentils, drained and rinsed

150ml (¼ pint) vegetable stock (see Top Tip)

a handful of rocket or lettuce leaves

salt and ground black pepper

1. Gently lower the eggs into a pan of boiling water and simmer for 7 minutes.

2. Meanwhile, heat the oil in a separate pan and fry the leeks, spring onions and red pepper for 6–8 minutes until softened.

3. Stir in the lentils and stock and bring to the boil, then reduce the heat and simmer for 1–2 minutes.

4. Peel the eggs, then cut in half. Season the lentil mixture with salt and pepper, then divide between two bowls and top each with an egg and a few rocket leaves.

TOP TIP
You can use ½ vegetable stock cube dissolved in 150ml (¼ pint) boiling water.

STAR QUALITIES
Ready in under 30 minutes
Healthy choice
Cheap eat
Brain food

CHICKEN DISHES

Easy Chicken & Vegetable Hotpot

Serves 4 • Preparation Time 5 minutes • Cooking Time 30 minutes • Per Serving 338 calories, 14g fat
(of which 3g saturates), 14g carbohydrate, 1.2g salt • Easy

**4 chicken breasts, with skin, about
   125g (4oz) each
2 large parsnips, chopped
2 large carrots, chopped
300ml (½ pint) ready-made gravy
125g (4oz) cabbage, shredded
ground black pepper**

1. Heat a non-stick frying pan or flameproof casserole until hot. Add the chicken breasts, skin side down, and cook for 5–6 minutes. Turn them over and add the parsnips and carrots. Cook for a further 7–8 minutes.

2. Pour the gravy over the chicken and vegetables, then cover and cook gently for 10 minutes.

3. Season with pepper and stir in the cabbage, then cover and continue to cook for 4–5 minutes until the chicken is cooked through, the cabbage has wilted and the vegetables are tender. Serve hot.

MONEYSAVER TIP
Leftovers can be turned into a hearty soup. Shred any cooked chicken and put into a pan with the vegetables. Add extra hot chicken stock and a drained can of mixed beans. Heat until piping hot.

STAR QUALITIES
*Healthy and sustaining
Comfort food
Share with friends*

Sticky Chicken Thighs

Serves 4 • Preparation Time 5 minutes • Cooking Time 20 minutes • Per Serving 218 calories, 12g fat (of which 3g saturates), 5g carbohydrate, 0.4g salt • Easy

1 garlic clove, peeled and crushed
1 tbsp clear honey
1 tbsp Thai sweet chilli sauce
4 chicken thighs
green salad to serve

1. Preheat the oven to 200°C (180°C fan oven) mark 6. Put the garlic into a bowl with the honey and chilli sauce and mix together. Add the chicken thighs and toss to coat.

2. Put into a roasting tin and roast for 15–20 minutes until the chicken is golden and cooked through. Serve with a crisp green salad.

TRY SOMETHING DIFFERENT
Try this with sausages instead of the chicken.

Italian Marinade
Mix 1 peeled and crushed garlic clove with 4 tbsp olive oil, the juice of 1 lemon and 1 tsp dried oregano. If you like, leave to marinate for 1–2 hours before cooking.

Oriental Marinade
Mix together 2 tbsp soy sauce, 1 tsp demerara sugar, 2 tbsp apple juice, 1 tsp finely chopped fresh root ginger and 1 peeled and crushed garlic clove.

Honey and Mustard
Mix together 2 tbsp grain mustard, 3 tbsp clear honey and the grated zest and juice of 1 lemon (see Top Tip, page 85).

STAR QUALITIES
Ready in under 30 minutes
Five ingredients or fewer
Cheap eat
Comfort food

Spicy Chicken Wings

Serves 4 • Preparation Time 5 minutes • Cooking Time 30–35 minutes • Per Serving 758 calories, 50g fat (of which 14g saturates), 0g carbohydrate, 0.6g salt • Easy

1 tbsp harissa paste (see Top Tip)
2 tsp ground cumin
1 tbsp olive oil
8 chicken wings
lemon wedges for squeezing
  (if you like)
salad to serve

1. Preheat the oven to 200°C (180°C fan oven) mark 6. Put the harissa, cumin and oil into a bowl and mix well.

2. Add the chicken wings and brush with the mixture. Put into a roasting tin and roast in the oven for 30–35 minutes until golden and tender.

3. Serve with lemon wedges, if you like, to squeeze over, and a salad.

TOP TIP
Harissa is a a spicy paste flavoured with chillies, coriander and caraway. You can use it with poultry, meat and fish, either when grilled, baked or in stews, so if you like spicy food, you will probably find plenty of uses for this North African spice blend. It's quite cheap to buy from supermarkets.

STAR QUALITIES
Healthy choice
Five ingredients or fewer
Share with friends
Great for parties

Fried Chicken

Serves 4 • Preparation Time 5 minutes • Cooking Time 35–45 minutes • Per Serving 565 calories, 42g fat (of which 10g saturates), 9g carbohydrate, 0.5g salt • Easy

4 chicken joints or pieces
3 tbsp plain flour
50g (2oz) butter or 3 tbsp
  vegetable oil
salt and ground black pepper
green salad to serve (if you like)

1. Wipe the chicken joints and pat dry with kitchen paper. Season with salt and pepper.

2. Toss the chicken in the flour until completely coated.

3. Heat the butter or oil in a large frying pan over a high heat. Add the chicken and cook until golden brown on both sides. Reduce the heat and cook for 30–40 minutes until tender. Drain on kitchen paper. Serve with a green salad, if you like.

TOP TIP
To make sure that the chicken stays moist, the surface should be browned at a high temperature to seal in all the juices and give a good colour; the heat should then be reduced for the remaining cooking time.

STAR QUALITIES
Five ingredients or fewer
Comfort food
Share with friends

One-pan Chicken with Tomatoes

Serves 4 • Preparation Time 5 minutes • Cooking Time 20–25 minutes • Per Serving 238 calories, 4g fat (of which 1g saturates), 20g carbohydrate, 1g salt • Easy

4 chicken thighs
1 red onion, peeled and sliced
400g can chopped tomatoes with herbs
400g can mixed beans, drained and rinsed
2 tsp balsamic vinegar
freshly chopped flat-leafed parsley to garnish (if you like)

1. Heat a non-stick pan and fry the chicken thighs, skin side down, until golden. Turn over and fry for 5 minutes.

2. Add the onion and fry for 5 minutes. Add the tomatoes, mixed beans and vinegar, cover and simmer for 10–12 minutes until piping hot. Garnish with chopped parsley, if you like, and serve immediately.

SWAP
Use flageolet, cannellini or haricot beans, or other canned beans, instead of mixed beans.

TOP TIP
If you don't have a non-stick pan, fry the chicken in 2 tbsp vegetable oil.

STAR QUALITIES
Quick and easy
Five ingredients or fewer
Cheap eat
Comfort food

Chicken, Bean & Spinach Curry

Serves 4 • Preparation Time 10 minutes • Cooking Time about 20 minutes • Per Serving 358 calories, 11g fat (of which 2g saturates), 38g carbohydrate, 2.9g salt • Easy

- 1 tbsp sunflower oil
- 350g (12oz) boneless, skinless chicken thighs, cut into strips
- 1 garlic clove, peeled and crushed
- 300–350g tub or jar curry sauce
- 400g can aduki beans, drained and rinsed
- 175g (6oz) ready-to-eat dried apricots
- 150g (5oz) natural yogurt, plus extra to serve
- 125g (4oz) baby spinach leaves (see Moneysaver Tips)
- naan bread to serve

1. Heat the oil in a large pan over a medium heat and fry the chicken strips with the garlic until golden. Add the curry sauce, beans and apricots, then cover and simmer gently for 15 minutes or until the chicken is tender.

2. Over a low heat, stir in the yogurt, keeping the curry hot without boiling it, then stir in the spinach until it just begins to wilt. Add a spoonful of yogurt and serve with naan bread.

MONEYSAVER TIPS

Instead of baby spinach leaves, use shredded spinach.

You could even make a very cheap vegetarian version using just the canned aduki beans. Use two cans to serve 4.

STAR QUALITIES

Healthy and sustaining
Comfort food
Share with friends
Great for parties

Chicken Chow Mein

Serves 4 • Preparation Time 10 minutes • Cooking Time 10 minutes • Per Serving 451 calories, 11g fat (of which 2g saturates), 59g carbohydrate, 1.3g salt • Easy

250g (9oz) medium egg noodles
1 tbsp toasted sesame oil
2 boneless, skinless chicken breasts or large thighs, cut into thin strips (see Moneysaver Tips)
1 bunch of spring onions, thinly sliced diagonally
150g (5oz) mangetouts, thickly sliced diagonally (see Moneysaver Tips)
125g (4oz) bean sprouts
100g (3½oz) cooked ham, shredded
120g sachet chow mein sauce
salt and ground black pepper
light soy sauce to serve

1. Cook the noodles in boiling water for 4 minutes or according to the pack instructions. Drain, rinse thoroughly in cold water, drain again and set aside.

2. Meanwhile, heat a wok or large frying pan until hot, then add the oil. Add the chicken and stir-fry over a high heat for 3–4 minutes until browned all over. Add the spring onions and mangetouts, stir-fry for 2 minutes, then stir in the bean sprouts and ham and cook for a further 2 minutes.

3. Add the drained noodles, then pour in the chow mein sauce and toss together to coat evenly. Stir-fry for 2 minutes or until piping hot. Season with salt and pepper and serve immediately with light soy sauce to drizzle over.

MONEYSAVER TIPS
Instead of boneless chicken, use chicken pieces and cut the meat off. Instead of mangetouts use frozen peas.

STAR QUALITIES
Ready in under 30 minutes
Healthy and sustaining
Share with friends

Chicken Stir-fry with Noodles

Serves 4 • Preparation Time 20 minutes • Cooking Time 20 minutes • Per Serving 355 calories, 10g fat
(of which 2g saturates), 29g carbohydrate, 0.5g salt • Easy

2 tbsp vegetable oil

2 garlic cloves, peeled and crushed

4 large skinless, boneless chicken thighs, each sliced into 10 pieces

3 medium carrots, peeled and cut into thin strips

250g pack thick egg noodles

1 bunch of spring onions, sliced

200g (7oz) mangetouts, ends trimmed

155g jar sweet chilli and lemongrass sauce

1. Fill a large pan with water and bring to the boil. Meanwhile, heat the oil in a wok or frying pan, then add the garlic and stir-fry for 1–2 minutes. Add the chicken pieces and stir-fry for 5 minutes, then add the carrot strips and stir-fry for a further 5 minutes.

2. Put the noodles into the boiling water and cook according to the pack instructions.

3. Meanwhile, add the spring onions, mangetouts and sauce to the wok and stir-fry for 5 minutes.

4. Drain the cooked noodles well and add to the wok. Toss everything together and serve.

STAR QUALITIES
Healthy and sustaining
Comfort food

FOOD FOR FRIENDS

Simple Chicken Casserole

Serves 4–6 • Preparation Time 5 minutes • Cooking Time 1¼–1½ hours • Per Serving 456 calories, 32g fat (of which 7g saturates), 10g carbohydrate, 1.7g salt • Easy

4–6 chicken joints
3 tbsp oil
1 onion, peeled and chopped
2 garlic cloves, peeled and crushed
2 celery sticks, chopped
2 carrots, peeled and chopped
1 tbsp plain flour
2 tbsp chopped fresh tarragon or
    thyme or 1 tsp dried
450ml (¾ pint) hot chicken stock
    (see Top Tips)
salt and ground black pepper

TOP TIPS
If you don't have a flameproof casserole, start everything off in a frying pan, then transfer to the casserole and put in the oven. You can use 1 chicken stock cube dissolved in 450ml (¾ pint) boiling water.

TIMESAVER TIP
Set the alarm on your mobile phone, or use a timer, and let the oven do the work while you get on with other things.

STAR QUALITIES
Healthy choice
Comfort food

1. Preheat the oven to 180°C (160°C fan oven) mark 4. Cut the chicken legs and breasts in half.

2. Heat the oil in a flameproof casserole and brown the chicken all over. Remove and pour off the excess oil. Add the onion and garlic and brown for a few minutes. Add the vegetables, then stir in the flour and cook for 1 minute. Add the herbs and seasoning, then add the chicken. Pour enough stock into the casserole to come three-quarters of the way up the chicken – you might not need it all, or you might need a little extra water. Cook in the oven for 1–1½ hours until the chicken is cooked through.

Lamb Chops with Crispy Garlic Potatoes

Serves 4 • Preparation Time 10 minutes • Cooking Time 20 minutes • Per Serving 835 calories, 45g fat (of which 19g saturates), 22g carbohydrate, 0.7g salt • Easy

2 tbsp mint sauce (see Top Tip)
8 small lamb chops
3 medium potatoes, peeled and cut
    into 5mm (¼in) slices
2 tbsp garlic-flavoured olive oil
1 tbsp olive oil
salt and ground black pepper
steamed green beans to serve

1. Spread the mint sauce over the lamb chops and leave to marinate while you prepare the potatoes.

2. Boil the potatoes in a pan of lightly salted water for 2 minutes until just starting to soften. Drain, tip back into the pan, season and toss through the garlic oil.

3. Meanwhile, heat the olive oil in a large frying pan and fry the chops for 4–5 minutes on each side until just cooked, adding a splash of boiling water to the pan to make a sauce. Remove the chops and sauce from the pan and keep warm.

4. Add the potatoes to the pan. Fry over a medium heat for 10–12 minutes until crisp and golden. Divide the potatoes, chops and sauce among four plates and serve with green beans.

TOP TIP
Mint sauce
Finely chop 20g (¾oz) fresh mint and mix with 1 tbsp each olive oil and white wine vinegar.

STAR QUALITIES
Ready in under 30 minutes
Quick and easy

Pork Chops with Apple Mash

Serves 4 • Preparation Time 5 minutes • Cooking Time about 15 minutes • Per Serving 532 calories, 26g fat (of which 11g saturates), 37g carbohydrate, 1.6g salt • Easy

4 large potatoes, peeled and chopped
4 tsp ready-made spice mix
4 pork chops
25g (1oz) butter
knob of butter
1 red apple, cored and chopped
salt and ground black pepper

1. Cook the potatoes in a pan of lightly salted water for 10–12 minutes until tender. Meanwhile, rub the spice mix into the pork chops.

2. Heat the butter in a pan. Add the chops and fry for 5 minutes on each side. Remove from the pan and put on warm plates. Add a splash of hot water to the pan and swirl the juices around to make a thin gravy. Drain the potatoes.

3. Melt a knob of butter in another pan. Add the apple and fry for 1–2 minutes until starting to soften. Tip the drained potatoes into the pan, season with salt and pepper and mash roughly with the apple. Serve with the chops and gravy.

STAR QUALITIES
Ready in under 30 minutes
Quick and easy
Comfort food

Spicy Pork Meatballs

Serves 4 • Preparation Time 15 minutes • Cooking Time about 35 minutes • Per Serving 324 calories, 15g fat (of which 4g saturates), 24g carbohydrate, 1.3g salt • Easy

FOR THE MEATBALLS

3 tbsp olive oil

400g (14oz) pork mince

½–1 red chilli, to taste, seeded and finely chopped (see Safety Tip, page 44)

½ tbsp wholegrain mustard

½ medium onion, peeled and finely chopped

1 medium egg

75g (3oz) fresh white breadcrumbs

salt and ground black pepper

boiled rice to serve

FOR THE SAUCE

1 tbsp olive oil

½ medium onion, peeled and finely chopped

½ tsp smoked or normal paprika

100ml (3½fl oz) red wine or beef stock

2 × 400g cans chopped tomatoes

fresh coriander or parsley to garnish (optional)

1. Preheat the oven to 200°C (180°C fan oven) mark 6. For the meatballs, pour the oil on to a lipped baking tray and put into the oven to heat up.

2. Put the mince, chilli, mustard, onion, egg, breadcrumbs and seasoning to taste into a large bowl. Use your hands to mix together, then roll into golfball-sized balls.

3. Using oven gloves, carefully take the tray out of the oven, add the meatballs and carefully roll them to coat in the oil. Put the tray back into the oven and cook for 25 minutes,

turning the balls occasionally, or until golden and cooked through.

4. Meanwhile, make the sauce. Heat the oil in a large pan and gently cook the onion for 10 minutes or until softened. Stir in the paprika and cook for 1 minute, then add the wine or stock and cook for 1 minute more. Stir in the tomatoes and leave to simmer for 15 minutes or until

the sauce is thick and pulpy. Check the seasoning.

5. Add the meatballs to the tomato sauce and cook for a further 5 minutes. Garnish with coriander or parsley, if you like, and serve with rice.

SWAP

If you want to make these meatballs healthier, use turkey instead of pork mince.

Grilled Lamb Steaks with Mixed Bean Salad

Serves 4 • Preparation Time 5 minutes • Cooking Time 10 minutes • Per Serving 545 calories, 20g fat (of which 7g saturates), 30g carbohydrate, 1.8g salt • Easy

150g (5oz) sunblush tomatoes in oil
1 garlic clove, peeled and crushed
2 rosemary sprigs
4 x 175g (6oz) leg of lamb steaks
½ small red onion, peeled and
**   finely sliced**
2 x 400g cans mixed beans,
**   drained and rinsed**
large handful of rocket
salt and ground black pepper

1. Preheat the grill to high. Drain the sunblush tomatoes, reserving the oil. Put the garlic into a large shallow dish with 1 tbsp oil from the tomatoes. Strip the leaves from the rosemary sprigs, snip into small pieces and add to the dish. Season with salt and pepper, then add the lamb and toss to coat.

2. Grill the lamb for 3–4 minutes on each side until cooked but still just pink. Meanwhile, roughly chop the tomatoes and put into a pan with the onion, beans, remaining rosemary, rocket and a further 1 tbsp oil from the tomatoes. Warm through until the rocket starts to wilt. Serve the lamb steaks with the bean salad on warmed plates.

STAR QUALITIES
Ready in under 30 minutes
Quick and easy
Healthy and sustaining
Comfort food

One-pot Spicy Beef

Serves 4 • Preparation Time 15 minutes • Cooking Time about 40 minutes • Per Serving 450 calories, 19g fat
(of which 7g saturates), 40g carbohydrate, 1.6g salt • Easy

2 tsp sunflower oil

**1 large onion, peeled and roughly
  chopped**

**1 garlic clove, peeled and finely
  chopped**

**1 small red chilli, seeded and
  finely chopped (see page 44)**

**2 red peppers, seeded and roughly
  chopped (see page 44)**

2 celery sticks, diced

400g (14oz) minced beef

400g can chopped tomatoes

**2 x 400g cans mixed beans,
  drained and rinsed**

1–2 tsp Tabasco

1. Heat the oil in a large frying
pan. Add the onion to the pan
with 2 tbsp water and cook for
10 minutes or until softened. Add
the garlic and chilli and cook for
1–2 minutes until golden, then add
the red peppers and celery and
cook for 5 minutes.

2. Add the mince and, as it browns,
use a wooden spoon to break up
the pieces. Add the tomatoes,
beans and Tabasco, then simmer
for 20 minutes.

TOP TIP

*For other recipes using minced
meat, see pages 118–119, 129,
172–173, 174.*

STAR QUALITIES

*Healthy and sustaining
Cheap eat
Comfort food*

Cottage Pie

Serves 4 • Preparation Time 15 minutes • Cooking Time 45 minutes • Per Serving 511 calories, 22g fat (of which 8g saturates), 53g carbohydrate, 1.8g salt • Easy

1 tbsp olive oil

1 onion, peeled and finely chopped

2 garlic cloves, peeled and crushed

450g (1lb) minced beef

1 tbsp plain flour

450ml (¾ pint) beef stock
(see Top Tip)

2 tbsp Worcestershire sauce

1 medium carrot, peeled and diced

125g (4oz) button mushrooms,
sliced

1kg (2¼lb) potatoes, mashed
(see step 3, page 174)

salt and ground black pepper

1. Heat the oil in a large pan, add the onion and fry over a medium heat for 15 minutes or until softened and golden, stirring occasionally. Add the garlic and cook for 1 minute.

2. Preheat the oven to 200°C (180°C fan oven) mark 6. Add the mince to the onion and garlic and, as it browns, use a wooden spoon to break up the pieces. Once it's brown, stir in the flour. Stir in the stock to the browned mince, cover the pan with a lid and bring to the boil. Add the Worcestershire sauce,

carrot and mushrooms and season well with salt and pepper.

3. Spoon the sauce into a 1.7 litre (3 pint) ovenproof dish, cover with the mashed potato, then cook in the oven for 20–25 minutes.

TOP TIP
You can use 1 beef stock cube dissolved in 450ml (¾ pint) boiling water.

STAR QUALITIES
Comfort food

Chilli con Carne

Serves 4 • Preparation Time 15 minutes • Cooking Time 40 minutes • Per Serving 397 calories, 22g fat
(of which 8g saturates), 22g carbohydrate, 2.5g salt • Easy

1 tbsp olive oil
1 onion, peeled and finely chopped
2 garlic cloves, peeled and crushed
1 red pepper, seeded and chopped
    (see page 44)
450g (1lb) minced beef
2 tsp chilli powder, mild or hot as
    you like
300ml (½ pint) beef stock
    (see Top Tip)
2 tbsp tomato purée
400g can chopped tomatoes
2 tbsp Worcestershire sauce
125g (4oz) button mushrooms,
    sliced

400g can red kidney beans, rinsed
    and drained
salt and ground black pepper
grated Cheddar cheese, rice or
    jacket potatoes or flour tortillas
    to serve (if you like)

1. Heat the oil in a large pan, add the onion and fry over a medium heat for 15 minutes or until softened and golden, stirring occasionally. Add the garlic and cook for 1 minute. Add the red pepper and cook for 5 minutes.

2. Add the mince and, as it browns, use a wooden spoon to break up the pieces. Stir in the chilli powder, stock and tomato purée to the browned mince, cover the pan with a lid and bring to the boil. Add the tomatoes, Worcestershire sauce and mushrooms and season well with salt and pepper. Bring back to the boil, then reduce the heat and simmer, stirring occasionally, for 15 minutes. Add the kidney beans and cook for a further 5 minutes to heat through. Grate some cheese over, if you like, then serve with either rice, jacket potato or tortillas.

TOP TIP
You can use 1 beef stock cube dissolved in 300ml (½ pint) boiling water.

STAR QUALITIES
Healthy and sustaining
Cheap eat
Comfort food

Shepherd's Pie

Serves 4 • Preparation Time 20 minutes • Cooking Time about 55 minutes • Per Serving 513 calories, 27g fat (of which 11g saturates), 44g carbohydrate, 0.6g salt • Easy

2 tbsp sunflower oil
450g (1lb) minced lamb
1 large onion, peeled and chopped
50g (2oz) mushrooms, sliced
2 carrots, peeled and chopped
2 tbsp plain flour
1 tbsp tomato purée
1 bay leaf, if you have it
300ml (½ pint) lamb stock
    (see Top Tip)
700g (1½lb) potatoes, peeled and
    cut into large chunks
25g (1oz) butter
60ml (2¼fl oz) milk
50g (2oz) Cheddar cheese,
    crumbled (if you like)

1. Heat half the oil in a large pan and brown the mince over a medium to high heat – do this in batches otherwise the meat will steam rather than fry. Remove with a slotted spoon on to a plate.

2. Turn the heat to low and add the remaining oil. Gently fry the onion, mushrooms and carrots for 10 minutes, or until softened. Stir in the flour and tomato purée and cook for 1 minute. Return the meat to the pan and add the bay leaf, if you have it. Pour in the stock and bring to the boil, then cover and simmer on a low heat for 25 minutes.

3. Preheat the oven to 200°C (180°C fan) mark 6. Cook the potatoes in lightly salted boiling water for 20 minutes, until tender. Drain and leave to stand in the colander for 2 minutes to steam dry. Melt the butter and milk in the potato pan and add the cooked potatoes. Mash until smooth.

4. Spoon the lamb mixture into a 1.7 litre (3 pint) casserole dish. Remove the bay leaf and check the seasoning. Cover with the mashed potato and sprinkle the cheese over, if you like. Bake for 15–20 minutes, until bubbling and golden. Serve immediately with green vegetables.

TOP TIP
You can use 1 lamb or vegetable stock cube dissolved in 300ml (½ pint) boiling water

STAR QUALITIES
Healthy and sustaining
Cheap eat
Comfort food

Beef Stroganoff

Serves 4 • Preparation Time 10 minutes • Cooking Time about 20 minutes • Per Serving 750 calories, 60g fat
(of which 35g saturates), 3g carbohydrate, 0.5g salt • Easy

**700g (1½lb) rump or fillet steak,
trimmed**

**50g (2oz) unsalted butter or 4 tbsp
olive oil**

1 onion, peeled and thinly sliced

**225g (8oz) brown-cap mushrooms,
sliced**

3 tbsp brandy (if you like)

1 tsp French mustard

**200ml (7fl oz) crème fraîche (see
Moneysaver Tip)**

100ml (3½fl oz) double cream

**3 tbsp freshly chopped flat-leafed
parsley**

salt and ground black pepper

**rice or noodles to serve (see pages
55 and 54)**

1. Cut the steak into strips about
5mm (¼in) wide and 5cm
(2in) long.

2. Heat half the butter or oil in a
large heavy frying pan over a
medium heat. Add the onion and
cook gently for 10 minutes or until
soft and golden. Remove with a
slotted spoon and put to one side.
Add the mushrooms to the pan and
cook, stirring, for 2–3 minutes until
golden brown; remove and put to
one side.

3. Increase the heat and add the
remaining butter or oil to the pan.
Quickly fry the meat, in two or
three batches, for 2–3 minutes,
stirring constantly to ensure even
browning. Remove from the pan.
Add the brandy, if you like, and
allow it to bubble to reduce.

4. Put all the meat, onion and
mushrooms back into the pan.
Reduce the heat and stir in the
mustard, crème fraîche and cream.
Heat through, stir in most of the
parsley and season with salt and
pepper. Serve with rice or noodles,
with the remaining parsley
scattered over the top.

MONEYSAVER TIP
*You can omit the crème fraîche
and increase the cream to 150ml
(¼ pint).*

STAR QUALITIES
*Quick and easy
Comfort food
Great for parties*

Fish & Chips

Serves 2 • Preparation Time 15 minutes • Cooking Time 12 minutes • Per Serving 1186 calories, 79g fat (of which 18g saturates), 73g carbohydrate, 3.2g salt • Easy

4 litres (7 pints) sunflower oil for deep-frying
125g (4oz) self-raising flour
¼ tsp baking powder
¼ tsp salt
1 medium egg
150ml (¼ pint) sparkling mineral water
2 hake fillets, about 125g (4oz) each
450g (1lb) Desirée potatoes, peeled and cut into 1cm (½in) chips
salt, vinegar and garlic mayonnaise to serve

SAFETY

Deep-frying with hot oil can be dangerous because the high heat means it can catch fire:
Use a pan with a lid.
Do not wear sleeves that can dangle in the oil.
Do not fill your pan more than half full.
Never put water in hot oil.
For advice on Kitchen Fires see page 19.

STAR QUALITIES

Ready in under 30 minutes
Quick and easy
Comfort food

1. Heat the oil in a deep-fryer to 190°C (test by frying a small cube of bread – it should brown in 20 seconds).

2. Whiz the flour, baking powder, salt, egg and water in a blender until combined into a batter. (Alternatively, put the ingredients into a bowl and beat everything together until smooth.) Drop one of the fish fillets into the batter to coat it.

3. Put half the chips in the deep-fryer, then add the battered fish. Fry for 6 minutes or until just cooked, then remove and drain well on kitchen paper. Keep warm if not serving immediately.

4. Drop the remaining fillet into the batter to coat, then repeat step 3 with the remaining chips. Serve with salt, vinegar and garlic mayonnaise.

Bacon & Tuna Hash

Serves 4 • Preparation Time 10 minutes • Cooking Time 35 minutes • Per Serving 359 calories, 21g fat (of which 7g saturates), 23g carbohydrate, 3.8g salt • Easy

450g (1lb) new potatoes, cut into small chunks

25g (1oz) butter

125g (4oz) streaky bacon rashers, cut into 2.5cm (1in) strips

1 large onion, peeled and roughly chopped

125g (4oz) pitted green or black olives (if you like)

200g can tuna in oil, drained and flaked

salt and ground black pepper

1. Put the potatoes into a pan of lightly salted water, bring to the boil, then reduce the heat and simmer, partially covered, for 5–10 minutes until beginning to soften. Drain and set aside.

2. Melt the butter in a non-stick frying pan, add the bacon and cook on a medium heat until beginning to brown, then add the onion. Cook for 5 minutes or until soft. Add the potatoes, and olives if you like, reduce the heat and cook for 10 minutes.

3. Using a spatula, turn the hash over and continue to cook for a further 10 minutes, turning every now and again. Add the tuna and cook for a further 4–5 minutes until the potatoes are done to the centre and the tuna is hot. Season to taste and serve.

STAR QUALITIES
Healthy choice
Cheap eat
Brain food
Comfort food

Stir-fried Salmon & Broccoli

Serves 2 • Preparation Time 10 minutes • Cooking Time 5–6 minutes • Per Serving 90 calories, 4g fat (of which 1g saturates), 9g carbohydrate, 2.7g salt • Easy

2 tsp sesame oil

1 red pepper, seeded and thinly sliced

½ red chilli, seeded and thinly sliced (see page 44)

1 garlic clove, peeled and crushed

125g (4oz) broccoli florets

2 spring onions, sliced

2 salmon fillets, about 125g (4oz) each, cut into strips

1 tsp Thai fish sauce (see Moneysaver Tip)

2 tsp soy sauce

wholewheat noodles to serve (see page 54)

1. Heat the oil in a wok or large frying pan. Add the red pepper, chilli, garlic, broccoli florets and spring onions and stir-fry over a high heat for 3–4 minutes.

2. Add the salmon fillets, Thai fish sauce and soy sauce and cook for 2 minutes, stirring gently. Serve immediately with noodles.

MONEYSAVER TIP

Instead of Thai fish sauce, season with a little salt.

STAR QUALITIES

Ready in under 30 minutes
Quick and easy
Healthy and sustaining
Brain food

Hot Noodle Salad

Serves 4 • Preparation Time 10 minutes • Cooking Time 5–7 minutes • Per Serving 396 calories, 14g fat
(of which 4g saturates), 52g carbohydrate, 0.5g salt • Easy

250g pack medium egg noodles

2 tsp groundnut oil

**2 × 300g packs stir-fry vegetables
(see Moneysaver Tip)**

1 tsp crushed chilli flakes

4 medium eggs, beaten

**roughly chopped peanuts, freshly
chopped coriander and lime
wedges to serve (if you like)**

1. Put the egg noodles into a bowl of boiling water and leave to soak for 5 minutes. Drain well.

2. Meanwhile, heat the oil in a large wok over a high heat. Add the vegetables and chilli flakes and stir-fry for 3–4 minutes. Season the eggs with salt and pepper and pour over the vegetables. Cook for 1–2 minutes to let the egg set on the bottom, then stir in the noodles.

3. Serve with roughly chopped peanuts, freshly chopped coriander and lime wedges to squeeze over the top, if you like.

Rice-stuffed Peppers

Serves 4 • Preparation Time 15 minutes • Cooking Time 55 minutes • Per Serving 208 calories, 5g fat (of which 1g saturates), 39g carbohydrate, 0g salt • Easy

225g (8oz) brown rice
1 tbsp olive oil
2 onions, peeled and chopped
400g can tomatoes (cherry tomatoes are good for this)
3 tbsp freshly chopped coriander, plus extra sprigs to garnish (if you like)
4 red peppers, halved and seeded, leaving stalks intact (see page 44)
150ml (¼ pint) hot vegetable stock (see Top Tips)

1. Preheat the oven to 200°C (180°C fan oven) mark 6. Cook the rice according to the pack instructions, then drain.

2. Meanwhile, heat the oil in a pan, add the onions and fry for 15 minutes. Add the tomatoes and leave to simmer for 10 minutes. Stir in the cooked rice and chopped coriander, then spoon the mixture into the halved peppers.

3. Put the peppers into a roasting tin and pour the stock around them. Cook in the oven for 30 minutes until tender. Serve sprinkled with coriander sprigs, if you like.

TOP TIPS

You can use ½ vegetable stock cube dissolved in 150ml (¼ pint) boiling water.
To make the dish into a complete meal add 50g (2oz) chopped blanched almonds or chopped cashew nuts to the cooked rice and coriander at step 2.

STAR QUALITIES

Healthy choice
Cheap eat

Mushrooms Stuffed with Couscous

Serves 4 • Preparation Time 3 minutes • Cooking Time about 12 minutes • Per Serving 340 calories, 21g fat (of which 9g saturates), 26g carbohydrate, 0.6g salt • Easy

125g (4oz) couscous (see Top Tip)
200ml (7fl oz) boiling water
20g pack fresh flat-leafed parsley, roughly chopped
280g jar mixed antipasti in oil, drained and oil put to one side
8 large flat mushrooms
25g (1oz) butter
25g (1oz) plain flour
300ml (½ pint) skimmed milk
75g (3oz) mature Cheddar, grated, plus extra to sprinkle
green salad to serve

1. Preheat the oven to 220°C (200°C fan oven) mark 7. Put the couscous into a bowl with the boiling water, the parsley, antipasti and 1 tbsp of the reserved oil. Stir well.

2. Put the mushrooms on a greased baking tray and spoon a little of the couscous mixture into the centre of each. Cook in the oven while you make the sauce.

3. Meanwhile, whisk together the butter, flour and milk in a small pan over a high heat until the mixture comes to the boil. Reduce the heat as soon as it starts to thicken, then whisk constantly until smooth. Take the pan off the heat and stir in the cheese.

4. Spoon the sauce over the mushrooms and sprinkle with the remaining cheese. Put back into the oven for a further 7–10 minutes until golden. Serve with a green salad.

STAR QUALITIES
Ready in under 30 minutes
Quick and easy
Healthy choice
Cheap eat

TOP TIP
Couscous
Often mistaken for a grain, couscous is actually a type of pasta that originated in North Africa. It is perfect for serving with stews and casseroles, or making into salads. The tiny pellets do not require cooking and can simply be soaked. Measure the couscous in a jug and add 1½ times the volume of hot water or stock. Cover the bowl and leave to soak for 5 minutes. Fluff up with a fork before serving. If using for a salad, leave the couscous to cool completely before adding the other salad ingredients.

EGGS

Courgette & Parmesan Frittata

Serves 4 • Preparation Time 10 minutes • Cooking Time 15–20 minutes • Per Serving 229 calories, 19g fat (of which 9g saturates), 2g carbohydrate, 0.6g salt • Easy

40g (1½oz) butter
1 small onion, peeled and finely chopped
225g (8oz) courgettes, trimmed and finely sliced
6 medium eggs, beaten
25g (1oz) Parmesan, freshly grated, plus shavings to garnish
salt and ground black pepper
green salad to serve

1. Melt 25g (1oz) butter in a small non-stick frying pan and cook the onion for about 10 minutes until softened. Add the courgettes and fry gently for 5 minutes or until they begin to soften.

2. Beat the eggs in a bowl and season with salt and pepper.

3. Add the remaining butter to the pan and heat, then pour in the eggs. Cook for 2–3 minutes until golden underneath and cooked around the edges. Meanwhile, preheat the grill to medium.

4. Sprinkle the grated cheese over the frittata and grill for 1–2 minutes until just set – make sure the handle doesn't get too hot. Scatter with Parmesan shavings, cut into quarters and serve with a green salad.

TRY SOMETHING DIFFERENT
Cherry Tomato & Rocket Frittata
Replace the courgettes with 175g (6oz) ripe cherry tomatoes, frying them for 1 minute only, until they begin to soften. Immediately after pouring in the eggs, scatter 25g (1oz) rocket leaves over the surface. Continue cooking as in step 3.

STAR QUALITIES
Quick and easy
Cheap eat
Brain food

Potato & Chorizo Tortilla

Serves 4 • Preparation Time 5 minutes • Cooking Time 25 minutes • Per Serving 431 calories, 32g fat (of which 7g saturates), 23g carbohydrate, 0.9g salt • Easy

6 tbsp olive oil

450g (1lb) potatoes, peeled and very thinly sliced

225g (8oz) onions, peeled and thinly sliced

2 garlic cloves, peeled and finely chopped

50g (2oz) sliced chorizo, cut into thin strips

6 large eggs, lightly beaten

salt and ground black pepper

1. Heat the oil in a small non-stick frying pan over a medium-low heat. Add the potatoes, onions and garlic. Stir together until coated in the oil, then cover the pan. Cook gently, stirring occasionally, for 10–15 minutes until the potato is soft. Season with salt, then add the chorizo.

2. Preheat the grill until hot. Season the beaten eggs with salt and pepper and pour over the potato mixture. Cook over a medium heat for 5 minutes or until beginning to brown at the edges and the egg is about three-quarters set. Put the pan under the grill to brown the top – make sure the handle doesn't get too hot. The egg should be a little soft in the middle, as it continues to cook and set as it cools.

3. Carefully loosen the tortilla around the edge and underneath with a knife or spatula. Cut into wedges and serve.

STAR QUALITIES

Quick and easy
Healthy choice
Cheap eat
Comfort food

Poached Eggs with Mushrooms

Serves 4 • Preparation Time 15 minutes • Cooking Time 20 minutes • Per Serving 276 calories, 23g fat (of which 9g saturates), 1g carbohydrate, 0.7g salt • Easy

8 medium-sized flat mushrooms

40g (1½oz) butter

8 medium eggs

225g (8oz) baby spinach leaves (see Moneysaver Tip)

4 tsp pesto (see Top Tip, page 90)

1. Preheat the oven to 200°C (180°C fan oven) mark 6. Arrange the mushrooms in a single layer in a small roasting tin and dot with the butter. Roast in the oven for 15 minutes or until golden brown and soft.

2. Meanwhile, bring a wide shallow pan of water to the boil. When the mushrooms are half-cooked and the water in the pan is bubbling furiously, break the eggs into the pan, spaced well apart, then take the pan off the heat. The eggs will take about 6 minutes to cook.

3. When the mushrooms are tender, put them on a warmed plate, cover and return to the turned-off oven to keep warm.

4. Put the roasting tin over a medium heat on the hob and add the spinach. Cook, stirring, for about 30 seconds until the spinach has just started to wilt.

5. The eggs should be set by now, so divide the mushrooms among four plates and top with a little spinach, a poached egg and a teaspoonful of pesto.

MONEYSAVER TIP
Intstead of baby spinach, use sliced spinach leaves.

STAR QUALITIES
Quick and easy
Five ingredients or fewer
Cheap eat
Brain food

Baked Eggs with Mushrooms

Serves 2 • Preparation Time 10 minutes • Cooking Time 15 minutes • Per Serving 238 calories, 21g fat (of which 5g saturates), 2g carbohydrate, 0.6g salt • Easy

2 tbsp olive oil
125g (4oz) mushrooms, chopped
225g (8oz) fresh spinach
2 medium eggs
2 tbsp single cream
salt and ground black pepper

1. Preheat the oven to 200°C (180°C fan oven) mark 6. Heat the oil in a large frying pan, add the mushrooms and stir-fry for 30 seconds. Add the spinach and stir-fry until wilted. Season to taste, then divide the mixture between two shallow ovenproof dishes.

2. Carefully break an egg into the centre of each dish, then spoon 1 tbsp single cream over each.

3. Cook in the oven for about 12 minutes until just set – the eggs will continue to cook a little once they're out of the oven. Grind a little more pepper over the top, if you like, and serve.

STAR QUALITIES
Ready in under 30 minutes
Quick and easy
Healthy choice

Chorizo Hash

Serves 4 • Preparation Time 10 minutes • Cooking Time 35–45 minutes • Per Serving 358 calories, 17g fat (of which 6g saturates), 34g carbohydrate, 0.9g salt • Easy

700g (1½lb) large floury potatoes, peeled and cut into large chunks
175g (6oz) chorizo sausage, in one piece, rind peeled off and discarded
1 large onion, peeled and finely chopped
4 medium eggs
salt

1. Preheat the oven to 200°C (180°C fan oven) mark 6. Cook the potatoes in lightly salted boiling water for 15–20 minutes until just tender. Drain well, then return to the pan and cover with a lid to keep them warm and dry off any moisture.

2. While the potatoes are cooking, cut the sausage into small dice, then fry in a roasting tin – no need to add any fat – over a high heat until it has turned a deep golden brown and is beginning to go crispy at the edges – about 15 minutes.

3. Remove the sausage from the tin with a fork or slotted spoon on to a plate and put to one side. Add the onion to the tin and fry over a medium heat for a good 10 minutes or until it turns golden brown. There should be enough oil from the sausage without having to add any extra oil.

4. Cut the cooked potatoes into smaller dice. Return the sausage and potatoes to the tin and cook over a medium heat for 5 minutes, without stirring, or until a golden crust forms on the bottom of the mixture. Break up the mixture, then cook again until another crust forms. Break up the mixture again and leave to cook for 2–3 minutes more.

5. Make four dips in the potato cake and crack an egg into each one. Cook in the oven for about 7 minutes until the egg whites are set but the yolks are still soft. Season the eggs with salt and serve at once.

STAR QUALITIES
Five ingredients or fewer
Cheap eat
Brain food
Comfort food

Creamy Baked Eggs

Serves 4 • Preparation Time 5 minutes • Cooking Time 15–18 minutes • Per Serving 153 calories, 14g fat
(of which 7g saturates), 1g carbohydrate, 0.2g salt • Easy

oil to grease
4 sun-dried tomatoes
4 medium eggs
4 tbsp double cream
salt and ground black pepper
bread to serve (Granary is good)

1. Preheat the oven to 180°C
(160°C fan oven) mark 4. Grease
four individual ramekins.

2. Put 1 tomato in each ramekin
and season with salt and pepper.
Carefully break an egg on top of
each, then drizzle 1 tbsp cream
over each egg.

3. Bake for 15–18 minutes –
the eggs will continue to cook
once they have been taken out
of the oven.

4. Leave to stand for 2 minutes
before serving. Serve with bread.

STAR QUALITIES

Quick and easy
Five ingredients or fewer
Cheap eat
Brain food

VEGGIES

Baked Jacket Potatoes

Serves 6 • Preparation Time 5 minutes • Cooking Time about 1½ hours • Per Serving 265 calories, 9g fat (of which 5g saturates), 43g carbohydrate, 0.8g salt • Easy

6 large baking potatoes, scrubbed
50–75g (2–3oz) butter
salt and ground black pepper

1. Preheat the oven to 200°C (180°C fan oven) mark 6. Prick the potatoes all over with a fork. Put them on a baking sheet and bake in the oven for 1½ hours or until the potatoes feel soft when gently squeezed, turning them over once.

2. When the potatoes are cooked, score a deep cross on each one, season with salt and pepper and top with a generous knob of butter to serve.

TIMESAVER TIP
Set the alarm on your mobile phone, or use a timer, and let the oven do the work while you get on with other things.

TRY SOMETHING DIFFERENT
Top the jacket potatoes with grated cheese, or crème fraîche and chopped chives, or soured cream and chopped spring onions.

STAR QUALITIES
Healthy and sustaining
Five ingredients or fewer
Cheap eat
Comfort food

Posh Jacket Potatoes

Serves 6 • Preparation Time 15–20 minutes • Cooking Time 1¼ hours • Per Serving 315 calories, 17g fat (of which 9g saturates), 38g carbohydrate, 1g salt • Easy

6 large baking potatoes, scrubbed
2 tbsp sunflower oil
1 tbsp coarse sea salt
4–5 large garlic cloves, unpeeled
50g (2oz) butter
6 tbsp crème fraîche
2 tbsp mustard seeds, toasted and
**   lightly crushed**
salt and ground black pepper
fresh oregano sprigs to garnish
**   (if you like)**

1. Preheat the oven to 200°C (180°C fan oven) mark 6. Prick the potato skins all over with a fork, rub with oil and sprinkle with salt. Cook in the oven for 1 hour. Twenty minutes before the end of the cooking time, put the garlic cloves into a small roasting tin and cook for 20 minutes.

2. Squeeze the potatoes gently to check they are well cooked, then remove the potatoes and garlic from the oven and leave to cool slightly. When cool enough to handle, slice the tops off the potatoes and scoop the flesh into a warm bowl. Squeeze the garlic out of its skin and add it to the potato flesh with the butter, crème fraîche and mustard seeds. Season to taste with salt and pepper, then mash well. Return the potato mixture to the hollowed skins.

3. Put the filled potatoes on a baking sheet, or into a baking tin, and return to the oven for 15 minutes or until golden brown. Garnish with oregano sprigs, if you like, and serve hot.

TIMESAVER TIP
Set the alarm on your mobile phone, or use a timer, and let the oven do the work while you get on with other things.

STAR QUALITIES
Cheap eat
Comfort food
Share with friends

Bubble & Squeak Cakes

Makes 12 • Preparation Time 15 minutes • Cooking Time 45 minutes, plus cooling • Per Cake 130 calories, 10g fat (of which 6g saturates), 10g carbohydrate, 0.2g salt • Easy

550g (1¼lb) old potatoes, peeled
125g (4oz) butter
175g (6oz) leeks, trimmed and finely shredded
175g (6oz) green cabbage, finely shredded
plain flour to dust
1 tbsp oil
salt and ground black pepper

1. Cook the potatoes in a large pan of lightly salted boiling water for about 20 minutes until tender, then drain and mash.

2. Heat 50g (2oz) butter in a large non-stick frying pan. Add the leeks and cabbage and fry for 5 minutes, stirring, or until soft and beginning to colour. Combine the leeks and cabbage with the potatoes and season well with salt and pepper. Leave to cool. When cool enough to handle, mould into 12 cakes and dust with flour.

3. Heat the oil and remaining butter in a non-stick frying pan and cook the cakes for 4 minutes on each side or until they are golden, crisp and hot right through. Serve.

STAR QUALITIES
Cheap eat
Comfort food

Buttered Cabbage

Serves 4 • Preparation Time 5 minutes • Cooking Time about 10 minutes • Per Serving 122 calories, 11g fat (of which 7g saturates), 4g carbohydrate, 0.2g salt • Easy

450g (1lb) finely shredded cabbage
½ tsp caraway seeds (optional)
50g (2oz) butter
juice of ½ lemon
salt

1. Cook the cabbage in lightly salted boiling water until just tender. Drain well.

2. Meanwhile, fry the caraway seeds, if you like, in a dry pan until toasted. Take the pan off the heat, add the butter and leave to melt in the heat of the pan.

3. Toss the butter through the cabbage and serve with the lemon juice.

STAR QUALITIES
Ready in under 30 minutes
Quick and easy
Healthy choice
Five ingredients or fewer

Green Beans & Flaked Almonds

Serves 4 • Preparation Time 5 minutes • Cooking Time 5–7 minutes • Per Serving 57 calories, 5g fat (of which trace saturates), 2g carbohydrate, 0g salt • Easy

200g (7oz) green beans
1 tsp olive oil
25g (1oz) flaked almonds
½ lemon

1. Bring a large pan of water to the boil. Add the green beans and cook for 4–5 minutes. Drain.

2. Meanwhile, heat the oil in a large frying pan. Add the almonds and cook for 1–2 minutes until golden. Turn off the heat, add the drained beans to the frying pan and toss. Squeeze over a little lemon juice just before serving.

TRY SOMETHING DIFFERENT
Use pinenuts instead of almonds, drizzle with balsamic vinegar and scatter with basil leaves to serve.

Buttery Runner Beans
Cook the beans as above, then drain well. Add a knob of butter and season well. Toss together and serve.

STAR QUALITIES
Quick and easy
Healthy choice
Five ingredients or fewer

Warm Broad Bean & Feta Salad

Serves 2 • Preparation Time 10 minutes • Cooking Time 5 minutes • Per Serving 321 calories, 22g fat (of which 8g saturates), 15g carbohydrate, 1.8g salt • Easy

225g (8oz) frozen broad beans
100g (3½oz) feta cheese, chopped
2 tbsp freshly chopped mint
2 tbsp extra virgin olive oil
a squeeze of lemon juice
salt and ground black pepper
lemon wedges to serve (if you like)

1. Cook the beans in lightly salted boiling water for 3–5 minutes until tender. Drain, then plunge into cold water and drain again.

2. Tip the beans into a bowl, add the feta cheese, mint, oil and a squeeze of lemon juice. Season well with salt and pepper and toss together. Serve with lemon wedges, if you like.

STAR QUALITIES
Ready in under 30 minutes
Quick and easy
Healthy choice

Roasted Mediterranean Vegetables

Serves 4 • Preparation Time 10 minutes • Cooking Time 35–40 minutes • Per Serving 252 calories, 18g fat (of which 3g saturates), 19g carbohydrate, 0.4g salt • Easy

4 tomatoes, halved
2 onions, peeled and quartered
4 red peppers, seeded and cut into
   strips (see page 44)
2 courgettes, trimmed and cut into
   thick slices
4 garlic cloves, unpeeled
6 tbsp olive oil
1 tbsp freshly chopped thyme
   leaves
salt and ground black pepper

1. Preheat the oven to 220°C (200°C fan oven) mark 7. Put the tomatoes into a large roasting tin with the onions, peppers, courgettes and garlic. Drizzle with the oil and sprinkle with thyme, salt and pepper.

2. Roast in the oven, turning occasionally, for 35–40 minutes until tender.

SWAP
Sprinkle with toasted sesame seeds and serve with hummus. Use oregano instead of thyme.

STAR QUALITIES
Healthy choice
Cheap eat
Comfort food
Share with friends

Charred Courgettes

Serves 4 • Preparation Time 5 minutes • Cooking Time 10 minutes • Per Serving 36 calories, 2g fat
(of which trace saturates), 2g carbohydrate, 0g salt • Easy

4 courgettes, halved lengthways
olive oil to brush
salt to sprinkle

1. Preheat the grill or barbecue, or use a griddle pan. Score a criss-cross pattern on the fleshy side of the courgettes. Brush lightly with oil and sprinkle with salt.

2. Cook the courgettes for 10 minutes or until just tender, turning them occasionally.

SWAP

Mix the olive oil with a good pinch of dried chilli flakes and a small handful of chopped fresh rosemary leaves.
Use a mixture of yellow and green courgettes, if you like.

STAR QUALITIES

Ready in under 30 minutes
Quick and easy
Healthy choice
Five ingredients or fewer

Roasted Vegetable Salad

Serves 4 • Preparation Time 15 minutes • Cooking Time 40 minutes • Per Serving 420 calories, 43g fat (of which 6g saturates), 5g carbohydrate, 1g salt • Easy

900g (2lb) mixed vegetables, such as fennel, courgettes, leeks, aubergines, baby turnips, new potatoes and red onions
2 garlic cloves, unpeeled
4–5 fresh marjoram or rosemary sprigs
5 tbsp olive oil
1 tsp flaked sea salt
mixed crushed peppercorns to taste
4 tsp balsamic vinegar
warm crusty bread to serve

FOR THE MUSTARD MAYONNAISE
150ml (¼ pint) mayonnaise
2 tbsp Dijon mustard
salt and ground black pepper

1. Preheat the oven to 220°C (200°C fan oven) mark 7. For the vegetables, quarter the fennel, chop the courgettes, leeks and aubergines and peel the turnips and onions, then cut the onions into wedges. Place the vegetables, garlic, marjoram or rosemary, the oil, salt and peppercorns in a roasting tin and toss well (see Top Tip).

2. Cook in the oven for 30–35 minutes until the vegetables are golden, tossing frequently. Sprinkle the vinegar over them and return to the oven for a further 5 minutes.

3. Make the mustard mayonnaise: mix together the mayonnaise and mustard, then season with salt and pepper and set aside.

4. Arrange the vegetable salad on a serving dish and serve with the mayonnaise and some crusty bread.

TOP TIP
It's best to roast vegetables in a single layer or they will steam and become soggy. Use two tins if necessary.

STAR QUALITIES
Quick and easy
Healthy choice
Cheap eat

Spinach with Tomatoes

Serves 6 • Preparation Time 10 minutes • Cooking Time 15 minutes • Per Serving 85 calories, 7g fat (of which 5g saturates), 3g carbohydrate, 0.3g salt • Easy

50g (2oz) butter
2 garlic cloves, peeled and crushed
450g (1lb) tomatoes, halved (baby plum tomatoes are good for this)
250g (9oz) baby spinach leaves (see Moneysaver Tip)
a large pinch of freshly grated nutmeg
salt and ground black pepper

1. Heat half the butter in a pan, add the garlic and cook until just soft. Add the tomatoes and cook for 4–5 minutes until just beginning to soften.

2. Put the spinach and a little water in a clean pan, cover and cook for 2–3 minutes until just wilted. Drain well, chop roughly and stir into the tomatoes.

3. Add the remaining butter and heat through gently. Season well with salt and pepper, stir in the nutmeg and serve.

MONEYSAVER TIP
Instead of baby spinach leaves, use shredded spinach.

STAR QUALITIES
Ready in under 30 minutes
Quick and easy
Healthy choice

MEAT-FREE MEALS

Getting the Balance Right

If you're a vegetarian or vegan, as with any diet, variety is all important. Provided a vegetarian diet includes a good range of cereals and grains, pulses, nuts and seeds, fruit and vegetables, dairy and/or soya products, it should be nutritionally sound. A small quantity of plant oils, margarine or butter is needed to provide essential fatty acids and vitamins.

Sources of protein

Most vegetarians needn't worry about getting enough protein: this nutrient is found in a wide variety of foods, including pulses, tofu and other soya bean products, Quorn, eggs, cheese, sprouted beans, nuts and seeds.

Meat substitutes

Pulses

These are all the various beans, peas and lentils. They are highly nutritious, especially when eaten with grains, such as couscous, pasta, rice or bread. Canned pulses are a convenient, quick alternative to soaking and cooking dried ones and most supermarkets stock a wide range. A 400g can (drained weight about 235g) is roughly equivalent to 100g (3½oz) dried beans. The dried beans double in weight after soaking.

Sprouted beans and seeds

These are rich in nutrients and lend a nutty taste and crunchy texture to salads and stir-fries. Fresh bean sprouts are available from most supermarkets.

Vegetarian cheeses

Most supermarkets and cheese shops now stock a range of vegetarian cheeses, produced using vegetarian rennet. See page 31.

Tofu

Also known as bean curd, tofu is made from ground soya beans. It is highly nutritious but virtually tasteless. However, it readily absorbs other flavours when marinated. It is available as firm, silken and smoked.

Tofu is sold as a chilled product and should be stored in the fridge. Once the packet is opened, the tofu should be kept immersed in a bowl of water in the fridge and eaten within four days.

Textured Vegetable Protein (TVP)

This forms the bulk of most ready-prepared vegetarian burgers, sausages and mince. It is made from a mixture of soya flour, flavourings and liquid. It has a slightly chewy, meat-like texture. TVP can be included in stews, pies, curries and other dishes, rather as meat would be used by non-vegetarians.

Quorn

The vegetarian product Quorn is derived from a distant relative of the mushroom and is a good source of complete protein for vegetarians. Like tofu, Quorn has a bland flavour and benefits from being marinated before cooking. Available from the chiller cabinet, Quorn should be kept in the fridge.

Quick Winter Minestrone

Serves 4 • Preparation Time 10 minutes • Cooking Time 45 minutes • Per Serving 334 calories, 11g fat (of which 3g saturates), 47g carbohydrate, 1.5g salt • Easy

2 tbsp olive oil

1 small onion, peeled and finely chopped

1 carrot, peeled and chopped

1 celery stick, chopped

1 garlic clove, peeled and crushed

2 tbsp chopped fresh thyme

1 litre (1¾ pints) hot vegetable stock (see Top Tip)

400g can chopped tomatoes

400g can borlotti beans, drained and rinsed

125g (4oz) minestrone pasta

175g (6oz) Savoy cabbage, shredded

salt and ground black pepper

pesto (see Top Tip, page 90), toasted ciabatta and extra virgin olive oil to serve (if you like)

1. Heat the oil in a large pan and add the onion, carrot and celery. Cook for 8–10 minutes until softened, then add the garlic and thyme and fry for another 2–3 minutes.

2. Add the hot stock, tomatoes and half the borlotti beans. Mash the remaining beans, stir into the soup and simmer for 30 minutes, adding the minestrone pasta and cabbage for the last 10 minutes of cooking time.

3. Check the seasoning, then serve the soup in individual bowls with a dollop of pesto on top and slices of toasted ciabatta drizzled with extra virgin olive oil on the side, if you like.

TOP TIP

You can use 2 vegetable stock cubes dissolved in 1 litre (1¾ pints) boiling water.

STAR QUALITIES

Healthy and sustaining
Cheap eat
Comfort food
Share with friends

Leek & Potato Pie

Serves 1 • Preparation Time 5 minutes • Cooking Time 25 minutes • Per Serving 474 calories, 22g fat (of which 13g saturates), 56g carbohydrate, 0.7g salt • Easy

2 medium potatoes, peeled and chopped
butter
1 large leek, chopped
25g (1oz) grated Cheddar cheese
salt and ground black pepper

1. Put the potatoes into a pan of lightly salted water, cover and bring to the boil. Simmer for 10–15 minutes until tender.

2. Meanwhile, heat a little butter in a frying pan. Add the leek and fry for 10–15 minutes until soft and golden. Preheat the grill.

3. Drain the potatoes and tip back into the pan. Season with salt and pepper, then mash with a small knob of butter. Put the leek into a small, ovenproof dish and cover with the mash. Top the pie with the cheese, then cook under the hot grill for 10 minutes or until hot and golden.

STAR QUALITIES
Healthy choice
Five ingredients or fewer
Cheap eat
Comfort food

Potato & Onion Pan Fry

Serves 4 • Preparation Time 5 minutes • Cooking Time 10–15 minutes • Per Serving 157 calories, 6g fat
(of which 1g saturates), 24g carbohydrate, 0.6g salt • Easy

**500g (1lb 2oz) potatoes, peeled
and thickly sliced**

2–3 tbsp olive oil

**1 onion, peeled and cut into
8 wedges**

**1 tbsp freshly chopped flat-leafed
parsley**

salt and ground black pepper

1. Put the potatoes into a pan of lightly salted boiling water and boil for 2–3 minutes. Meanwhile, heat the oil in a pan and fry the onion for 5 minutes. Drain the potatoes and add to the pan.

2. Cook for 5–10 minutes until golden and crisp, then season well and toss the parsley through to serve.

TOP TIP

To make this dish into a complete meal, serve with fried or hardboiled eggs, baked beans or red kidney beans in chilli sauce.

STAR QUALITIES

Ready in under 30 minutes
Quick and easy
Five ingredients or fewer
Cheap eat

Cauliflower Cheese

Serves 2 • Preparation Time 5 minutes • Cooking Time 20 minutes • Per Serving 383 calories, 24g fat (of which 14g saturates), 20g carbohydrate, 2.2g salt • Easy

1 cauliflower
1 quantity cheese sauce
   (see page 23)
extra grated cheese to sprinkle
salt

1. Preheat the grill. Remove the coarse outer leaves from the cauliflower, cut a cross in the stalk end and give the whole cauliflower a good wash under the tap.

2. Put the cauliflower into a medium pan, with the stem side down, then pour over enough boiling water to come halfway up it. Add a pinch of salt and cover the pan. Bring to the boil and cook for 10–15 minutes. Stick a sharp knife into the florets – they should be tender but not mushy.

3. Drain the cauliflower and put it into an ovenproof dish. Pour the cheese sauce over it, sprinkle with a little grated cheese, then grill for 2–3 minutes until golden on top. Serve on its own or with a jacket potato.

TRY SOMETHING DIFFERENT
Make this with ½ head of cauliflower and ½ head of broccoli. Cut the stems off the florets, then peel and chop them into pieces the same size as the cauliflower and broccoli florets. They will take only about 4 minutes to cook until just tender. Make as above.

STAR QUALITIES
Quick and easy
Healthy choice
Five ingredients or fewer
Cheap eat

Peppers Stuffed with Mushrooms

Serves 4 • Preparation Time 20 minutes • Cooking Time about 50 minutes • Per Serving 375 calories, 25g fat (of which 11g saturates), 27g carbohydrate, 1.5g salt • Easy

40g (1½oz) butter

4 red peppers, halved and seeded, leaving the stalks intact (see page 44)

3 tbsp olive oil

350g (12oz) chestnut mushrooms, roughly chopped

4 tbsp freshly chopped chives

100g (3½oz) feta cheese

50g (2oz) fresh white breadcrumbs

25g (1oz) freshly grated Parmesan

salt and ground black pepper

1. Preheat the oven to 180°C (160°C fan oven) mark 4. Use a little of the butter to grease a shallow ovenproof dish, then put in the peppers side by side, hollow side up.

2. Heat the remaining butter and 1 tbsp of the oil in a pan. Add the mushrooms and fry until they are golden and there's no excess liquid left in the pan. Stir in the chives, then spoon the mixture into the pepper halves.

3. Crumble the feta cheese over the mushrooms. Mix the breadcrumbs and Parmesan in a bowl, then sprinkle the mixture over the top.

4. Season with salt and pepper and drizzle with the remaining oil. Roast for 45 minutes or until golden and tender. Serve warm.

STAR QUALITIES
Healthy choice
Cheap eat
Comfort food
Share with friends

Cheese & Vegetable Bake

Serves 4 • Preparation Time 15 minutes • Cooking Time 15 minutes • Per Serving 471 calories, 13g fat (of which 7g saturates), 67g carbohydrate, 0.8g salt • Easy

250g (9oz) macaroni

1 cauliflower, cut into florets (see page 46)

2 leeks, finely chopped

100g (3½oz) frozen peas

25g (1oz) wholemeal breadcrumbs

crusty bread to serve

FOR THE CHEESE SAUCE

15g (½oz) butter

15g (½oz) plain flour

200ml (7fl oz) skimmed milk

75g (3oz) freshly grated Parmesan (see Top Tip)

2 tsp Dijon mustard

salt and ground black pepper

1. Cook the macaroni in a large pan of boiling water for 6 minutes, adding the cauliflower and leeks for the last 4 minutes and the peas for the last 2 minutes.

2. Meanwhile, make the cheese sauce. Melt the butter in a pan and add the flour. Cook for 1–2 minutes, then take off the heat and gradually stir in the milk. Put back on the hob and bring to the boil slowly, stirring until the sauce thickens. Stir in 50g (2oz) Parmesan and the mustard. Season to taste with salt and pepper.

3. Preheat the grill to medium. Drain the pasta and the vegetables and put back in the pan. Add the cheese sauce and mix well. Spoon into a large shallow 2 litre (3½ pint) ovenproof dish and scatter the remaining Parmesan and the breadcrumbs over. Grill for 5 minutes or until golden and crisp. Serve hot with bread.

TOP TIP

A wide range of vegetarian cheeses is available, see page 31.

STAR QUALITIES

Quick and easy
Healthy choice
Cheap eat
Comfort food

Roasted Ratatouille

Serves 6 • Preparation Time 15 minutes • Cooking Time 1½ hours • Per Serving 224 calories, 18g fat (of which 3g saturates), 14g carbohydrate, 0.4g salt • Easy

400g (14oz) red peppers, seeded and roughly chopped (see page 44)
700g (1½lb) aubergines, stalk removed, cut into chunks
450g (1lb) onions, peeled and cut into wedges
4 or 5 garlic cloves, unpeeled and left whole
150ml (¼ pint) olive oil
1 tsp fennel seeds (if you like)
200ml (7fl oz) passata sauce (puréed and sieved tomatoes, available in jars, see Moneysaver Tip)
salt and ground black pepper
a few fresh thyme sprigs to garnish (if you like)

1. Preheat the oven to 240°C (220°C fan oven) mark 9. Put the peppers, aubergine, onions, garlic, oil and fennel seeds, if you like, into a roasting tin. Season with salt and pepper and toss together.

2. Put into the oven and cook for 30 minutes (tossing frequently during cooking) or until the vegetables are charred and beginning to soften.

3. Using oven gloves, carefully remove the tin from the oven. Stir the passata through the vegetables, then put the roasting tin back in the oven for another 50–60 minutes, stirring occasionally. Garnish with the thyme sprigs, if you like, and serve.

MONEYSAVER TIP
Instead of passata, blend 200g (7oz) canned tomatoes.

TOP TIP
To make the dish into a complete meal, stir in 2 ×160g packs smoked or marinated tofu chunks after 30 minutes of cooking time.

TIMESAVER TIP
Set the alarm on your mobile phone, or use a timer, and let the oven do the work while you get on with other things.

Grilled Sweet Potatoes with Feta & Olives

Serves 4 • Preparation Time 15 minutes • Cooking Time 15–20 minutes • Per Serving 324 calories, 23g fat (of which 9g saturates), 21g carbohydrate, 2.5g salt • Easy

1 large sweet potato, weighing about 500g (1lb 2oz)

4 tbsp olive oil, plus extra to brush

200g (7oz) feta cheese

2 tsp dried mixed herbs

50g (2oz) pitted black olives, chopped

1 garlic clove, peeled and crushed

salt and ground black pepper

flat-leafed parsley sprigs to garnish (if you like)

1. Preheat the barbecue or grill. Peel the sweet potato and cut lengthways into eight wedges. Put them into a pan of boiling water and bring back to the boil, then reduce the heat and simmer for 3 minutes. Drain and put in cold water. Drain again, dry well on kitchen paper, then brush lightly with oil. Season with salt and pepper, then barbecue or grill for 10–15 minutes until well browned and cooked through.

2. Meanwhile, mash the cheese, herbs, olives, garlic and the 4 tbsp oil together. Serve the sweet potato with the feta cheese mixture, garnished with flat-leafed parsley, if you like.

STAR QUALITIES

Healthy choice
Cheap eat
Comfort food
Share with friends

Thai Vegetable Curry

Serves 4 • Preparation Time 15 minutes • Cooking Time 15 minutes • Per Serving 203 calories, 12g fat (of which 2g saturates), 16g carbohydrate, 0.6g salt • Easy

2–3 tbsp Thai red curry paste (see Top Tip)

2.5cm (1in) piece fresh root ginger, peeled and finely chopped

50g (2oz) cashew nuts

400ml can coconut milk

3 carrots, peeled and cut into thin batons

1 broccoli head, cut into florets (see page 46)

20g (¾oz) fresh coriander, roughly chopped

zest and juice of 1 lime

2 large handfuls of washed spinach leaves

basmati rice to serve

1. Put the curry paste into a large pan. Add the ginger to the pan with the cashew nuts. Stir over a medium heat for 2–3 minutes.

2. Add the coconut milk, cover and bring to the boil. Stir the carrots into the pan and simmer for 5 minutes, then add the broccoli florets and simmer for a further 5 minutes or until the vegetables are tender.

3. Stir the coriander and lime zest into the pan with the spinach. Squeeze the lime juice over and serve with basmati rice.

TOP TIP
Not all curry pastes are vegetarian, so check the label.

STAR QUALITIES
Healthy choice
Cheap eat
Comfort food
Share with friends

Chilli Onions with Goat's Cheese

Serves 6 • Preparation Time 15 minutes • Cooking Time 45 minutes • Per Serving 276 calories, 23g fat
(of which 16g saturates), 5g carbohydrate, 0.9g salt • Easy

75g (3oz) unsalted butter, softened
2 medium red chillies, seeded and
    finely chopped (see page 44)
1 tsp dried chilli flakes
6 small red onions, peeled
3 x 100g (3½oz) goat's cheese logs,
    with rind
salt and ground black pepper
balsamic vinegar to serve

1. Preheat the oven to 200°C (180°C fan oven) mark 6. Put the butter in a small bowl, beat in the fresh and dried chillies and season well with salt and pepper.

2. Cut off the root from one of the onions, sit it on its base, then make several deep cuts in the top to create a star shape, slicing about two-thirds of the way down the onion. Do the same with the other five onions, then divide the chilli butter equally among them, pushing it down into the cuts.

3. Put the onions in a small roasting tin, cover with foil and bake for 40–45 minutes until soft. About 5 minutes before they are ready, slice each goat's cheese in two, leaving the rind intact, then put on a baking sheet and bake for 2–3 minutes. To serve, put each onion on top of a piece of goat's cheese and drizzle with balsamic vinegar.

STAR QUALITIES
Share with friends
Great for parties

Potato & Broccoli Curry

Serves 4 • Preparation Time 20 minutes • Cooking Time about 40 minutes • Per Serving 302 calories, 10g fat (of which 1g saturates), 46g carbohydrate, 0.5g salt • Easy

600g (1lb 5oz) new potatoes, scrubbed and cut into bite-size cubes

2 tbsp sunflower oil

2 onions, peeled and sliced

400g can chickpeas, drained and rinsed

250ml (9fl oz) hot vegetable stock (see Top Tips)

150g (5oz) chopped broccoli (see page 46)

salt and ground black pepper

2 tbsp each mango chutney and Greek yogurt, mixed together, and naan bread to serve

FOR THE SPICE MIX

2 tsp ground cumin

2 tsp paprika

1 tsp ground coriander

finely grated zest of ½ orange (see Top Tip, page 85)

1. Cook the potatoes in a pan of lightly salted boiling water for 5 minutes, then drain.

2. Meanwhile, stir the spice mix ingredients together with a good pinch of salt. Dry-fry the spice mix for 2–3 minutes in a large frying pan, then add the oil and onions and fry for 7–8 minutes until soft and golden.

3. Add the potatoes, chickpeas and hot stock. Season to taste with salt and pepper, then cook for 15–20 minutes, adding the broccoli for the last 4–5 minutes of cooking time. Serve with the mango chutney, yogurt and naan bread.

TOP TIPS
You could use any canned pulses in this curry, such as butter beans, black-eyed peas or brown lentils. You can use 1 vegetable stock cube dissolved in 250ml (9fl oz) boiling water.

STAR QUALITIES
*Healthy and sustaining
Cheap eat
Comfort food
Share with friends*

Saag Aloo

Serves 4 • Preparation Time 15 minutes • Cooking Time 55 minutes • Per Serving 295 calories, 10g fat (of which 1g saturates), 47g carbohydrate, 0.2g salt • Easy

2–3 tbsp vegetable oil
1 onion, peeled and finely sliced
2 garlic cloves, peeled and finely chopped
1 tbsp black mustard seeds
2 tsp ground turmeric
900g (2lb) potatoes, peeled and cut into chunks
1 tsp salt
4 handfuls of baby spinach leaves (see Moneysaver Tip)

1. Heat the oil in a pan and fry the onion over a medium heat for 10 minutes or until golden, taking care not to burn it.

2. Add the garlic, mustard seeds and turmeric and cook for 1 minute. Add the potatoes, salt and 150ml (¼ pint) water. Cover the pan, bring to the boil, then reduce the heat and cook gently for 35–40 minutes until tender. Add the spinach and cook until the leaves just wilt. Serve immediately.

MONEYSAVER TIP
Instead of baby spinach leaves, use shredded spinach.

TOP TIP
To make the curry into a complete meal, add 400g can chickpeas or other beans, drained and rinsed, then cook for 5–10 minutes before adding the spinach.

STAR QUALITIES
Healthy choice
Cheap eat
Comfort food
Share with friends

Veggie Curry

Serves 1 • Preparation Time 5 minutes • Cooking Time 12 minutes • Per Serving 299 calories, 10g fat (of which 1g saturates), 32g carbohydrate, 2.3g salt • Easy

1 tbsp medium curry paste (see Top Tip, page 213)
227g can chopped tomatoes
150ml (¼ pint) hot vegetable stock (see Top Tip)
200g (7oz) vegetables, such as broccoli, courgettes and sugarsnap peas, roughly chopped
½ × 400g can chickpeas, drained and rinsed
griddled wholemeal pitta and yoghurt to serve

1. Heat the curry paste in a large heavy-based pan for 1 minute, stirring the paste to warm the spices. Add the tomatoes and hot stock. Bring to the boil, then reduce the heat to a simmer and add the vegetables. Simmer for 5–6 minutes until the vegetables are tender.

2. Stir in the chickpeas and heat for 1–2 minutes until hot. Serve the vegetable curry with a griddled wholemeal pitta and yogurt.

TOP TIP
You can use ½ vegetable stock cube dissolved in 150ml (¼ pint) boiling water.

STAR QUALITIES
Ready in under 30 minutes
Healthy and sustaining
Comfort food
Share with friends

SWEET THINGS

Orange Eggy Bread

Serves 4 • Preparation Time 10 minutes • Cooking Time 15 minutes • Per Serving 358 calories, 13g fat (of which 7g saturates), 54g carbohydrate, 1.2g salt • Easy

2 large eggs
150ml (¼ pint) milk
finely grated zest of 1 orange
    (see Top Tip, page 85)
50g (2oz) butter
8 slices raisin bread, halved
    diagonally
1 tbsp caster sugar
vanilla ice cream and orange
    segments to serve

1. Lightly whisk the eggs, milk and orange zest together in a bowl.

2. Heat the butter in a large frying pan over a medium heat. Dip the slices of raisin bread into the egg mixture and fry on both sides until golden.

3. Sprinkle the bread with the sugar and serve immediately with ice cream and orange slices.

STAR QUALITIES
Ready in under 30 minutes
Quick and easy
Cheap eat
Comfort food

Sweet Kebabs

Serves 4 • Preparation Time 5 minutes • Cooking Time 3 minutes • Per Serving 521 calories, 23g fat (of which 12g saturates), 77g carbohydrate, 0.3g salt • Easy

chocolate brownie, about 10 x 5cm (4 x 2in), cut into eight chunks
8 large strawberries
whipped cream to serve

1. Preheat the grill or barbecue. Spear alternate chunks of chocolate brownie and strawberries on to skewers. Grill or barbecue for 3 minutes, turning occasionally. Serve with whipped cream.

STAR QUALITIES
Ready in under 30 minutes
Quick and easy
Five ingredients or fewer
Cheap eats

Strawberry & Chocolate Muffins

Serves 4 • Preparation Time 5 minutes • Per Serving 420 calories, 20g fat (of which 12g saturates), 55g carbohydrate, 0.6g salt • Easy

2 chocolate muffins, halved
4 tbsp mascarpone or cream
   cheese, softened
600g (1lb 5oz) strawberries, hulled
   and roughly chopped
plain chocolate, grated, to decorate

1. Divide the muffin halves among four plates. Top each half with a tablespoon of the cheese and a good spoonful of strawberries.

2. Sprinkle with the grated chocolate and serve immediately.

STAR QUALITIES
Ready in under 30 minutes
Quick and easy
Five ingredients or fewer
Comfort food

Cherry Yogurt Crush

Serves 4 • Preparation Time 10 minutes, plus chilling • Per Serving 390 calories, 18g fat
(of which 9g saturates), 45g carbohydrate, 0.5g salt • Easy

**400g can stoned cherries, drained,
or 450g (1lb) fresh cherries,
stoned**
500g (1lb 2oz) Greek yogurt
**150g (5oz) macaroons (see
Moneysaver Tip)**

1. Spoon some cherries into the bottom of each of four 400ml (14fl oz) glasses. Top with a dollop of yogurt and some biscuits. Continue layering up each glass until all the ingredients have been used.

2. Chill for 15 minutes to 2 hours before serving.

MONEYSAVER TIP
Instead of macaroons use broken HobNobs or shortbread biscuits.

STAR QUALITIES
Quick and easy
Five ingredients or fewer
Comfort food
Share with friends

Fruity Fool

Serves 6 • Preparation Time 2 minutes • Per Serving 159 calories, 2g fat (of which trace saturates), 31g carbohydrate, 0.1g salt • Easy

500g carton summer fruit compôte
500g carton fresh custard

1. Divide half the compôte among six glasses, then add a thin layer of custard. Repeat the process until all the compôte and custard have been used.

2. Stir each fool once to swirl the custard and compôte together, then serve.

STAR QUALITIES
Ready in under 30 minutes
Quick and easy
Five ingredients or fewer
Cheap eat

Lemon & Passion Fruit Fool

Serves 6 • Preparation Time 20 minutes • Per Serving 210 calories, 17g fat (of which 10g saturates), 14g carbohydrate, 0.1g salt • Easy

6 tbsp lemon curd
4 ripe passion fruits
150ml (¼ pint) double cream
1 tbsp icing sugar
200g (7oz) Greek yogurt
toasted flaked almonds to decorate

1. Put the lemon curd into a small bowl. Halve the passion fruits and spoon the pulp into a sieve resting over a bowl. Stir to separate the seeds from the juice. Add 1 tbsp of the passion fruit juice to the lemon curd and mix well.

2. In a large bowl, whip the cream with the icing sugar until soft peaks form. Stir in the yogurt.

3. Put a dollop of yogurt cream into each of six small glasses. Layer with a spoonful of lemon curd mixture and 1 tsp passion fruit juice. Repeat to use up all the ingredients. Scatter some toasted flaked almonds on top and serve immediately.

STAR QUALITIES
Ready in under 30 minutes
Quick and easy
Comfort food
Share with friends

Quick Lemon Mousse

Serves 4 • Preparation Time 1–2 minutes • Per Serving 334 calories, 30g fat (of which 18g saturates), 16g carbohydrate, 0.1g salt • Easy

6 tbsp lemon curd
300ml (½ pint) double cream, whipped
fresh berries to decorate

1. Gently stir the lemon curd through the double cream until combined and decorate with berries.

STAR QUALITIES

Ready in under 30 minutes
Quick and easy
Five ingredients or fewer
Cheap eat

Cheat's Chocolate Pots

Serves 4 • Preparation Time 5 minutes, plus chilling • Cooking Time 5 minutes • Per Serving 385 calories, 17g fat (of which 9g saturates), 53g carbohydrate, 0.1g salt • Easy

500g carton fresh custard
200g (7oz) plain chocolate, broken into pieces

1. Put the custard into a small pan with the chocolate pieces. Heat gently, stirring all the time, until the chocolate has melted.

2. Pour the mixture into four small cups or glasses and chill in the fridge for 30 minutes to 1 hour before serving.

TRY SOMETHING DIFFERENT
Serve the mixture warm as a sauce for vanilla ice cream.

STAR QUALITIES
Quick and easy
Five ingredients or fewer
Cheap eat
Comfort food

Grilled Coconut Cake

Serves 4 • Preparation Time 5 minutes • Cooking Time 5 minutes • Per Serving 434 calories, 24g fat
(of which 0g saturates), 51g carbohydrate, 1g salt • Easy

4 thick slices coconut or Madeira cake
icing sugar to dust
Greek yogurt or crème fraîche and fresh fruit to serve

1. Preheat the grill. Grill the cake until lightly charred on both sides. Dust with icing sugar and serve with thick Greek yogurt and fresh fruit, cut into bite-size pieces.

STAR QUALITIES
Ready in under 30 minutes
Quick and easy
Cheap eat
Comfort food

Roasted Apples with Oats & Blueberries

Serves 4 • Preparation Time 15 minutes • Cooking Time 30–40 minutes • Per Serving 164 calories, 5g fat (of which trace saturates), 29g carbohydrate, 0g salt • Easy

4 cooking apples (see Top Tip)
25g (1oz) pecan nuts, chopped
25g (1oz) rolled (porridge) oats
50g (2oz) blueberries
2 tbsp light muscovado sugar
4 tbsp orange juice

1. Preheat the oven to 200°C (180°C fan oven) mark 6. Core the apples, then use a sharp knife to score around the middle of each (this will stop the apple from collapsing). Put the apples into a roasting tin.

2. Put the pecan nuts into a bowl together with the oats, blueberries and sugar. Mix together, then spoon into the apples, pour 1 tbsp orange juice over each apple and

bake in the oven for 30–40 minutes until the apples are soft.

TOP TIP
Apples are easy to work with because they are very firm-fleshed, but their flesh turns brown when exposed to air and starts to discolour quickly. Toss with lemon juice if you are not going to use the prepared fruit immediately.

STAR QUALITIES
Comfort food
Share with friends

Cinnamon Pancakes

Serves 6 • Preparation Time 5 minutes • Cooking Time 20 minutes • Per Serving 141 calories, 5g fat (of which 1g saturates), 20g carbohydrate, 0.1g salt • Easy

150g (5oz) plain flour
½ tsp ground cinnamon
1 medium egg
300ml (½ pint) skimmed milk
olive oil to fry
fruit compôte or sugar and Greek
** yogurt to serve**

1. Put the flour, cinnamon, egg and milk into a large bowl and whisk together to make a smooth batter. Leave to stand for 20 minutes.

2. Heat a heavy-based frying pan over a medium heat. When the pan is really hot, add 1 tsp oil, pour in a ladleful of batter and tilt the pan to coat the bottom of the pan with an even layer of batter. Cook for 1 minute or until golden. Flip the pancake over and cook for 1 minute. Remove the pancake from the pan and put on to a

warmed plate. Repeat with the remaining batter, adding more oil if necessary, to make six pancakes. Serve with a fruit compôte or a sprinkling of sugar, and a dollop of yogurt.

TRY SOMETHING DIFFERENT

Sprinkle the cooked pancakes with caster sugar and squeeze lemon juice over.
Spread the pancakes with 1 tbsp chocolate spread and top with sliced banana.
Serve with sliced bananas and vanilla ice cream instead of the fruit compôte and yogurt.

STAR QUALITIES

Ready in under 30 minutes
Quick and easy
Cheap eat
Comfort food

Quick Chocolate Slices

Makes 40 • Preparation Time 10 minutes, plus chilling • Cooking Time 2 minutes • Per Serving 137 calories,
9g fat (of which 6g saturates), 13g carbohydrate, 0.3g salt • Easy

225g (8oz) butter or olive oil spread

3 tbsp golden syrup

50g (2oz) cocoa, sifted

**300g pack digestive biscuits,
crushed**

**400g (14oz) plain chocolate, broken
into pieces**

1. Put the butter or olive oil spread in a heatproof bowl and add the golden syrup and cocoa. Melt in a 900W microwave on full power for 20 seconds or until melted, or melt in a pan over a very low heat. Mix everything together.

2. Remove from the heat and stir in the biscuits. Mix well until thoroughly coated in chocolate, crushing down any large pieces of biscuit.

3. Turn into a greased 25.5 x 16.5cm (10 x 6½in) rectangular tin. Cool, cover and chill for 20 minutes.

4. Melt the chocolate in a heatproof bowl in a 900W microwave on full power for 1 minute 40 seconds, stirring twice. Or, put the bowl over a pan of gently simmering water, making sure the base of the bowl doesn't touch the water, and leave until melted. Stir once more and pour over the chocolate biscuit base, then chill for 20 minutes. Cut in half lengthways and cut each half into 20 rectangular fingers.

STAR QUALITIES
Five ingredients or fewer
Comfort food
Share with friends
Great for parties

Pear & Blackberry Crumble

Serves 6 • Preparation Time 20 minutes • Cooking Time 35–45 minutes • Per Serving 525 calories, 21g fat (of which 9g saturates), 81g carbohydrate, 0.3g salt • Easy

450g (1lb) pears, peeled, cored and chopped, tossed with the juice of 1 lemon (see Top Tip, page 229)

225g (8oz) golden caster sugar

1 tsp mixed spice

450g (1lb) blackberries

cream, custard or ice cream to serve

FOR THE CRUMBLE TOPPING

100g (3½oz) butter, chopped, plus extra to grease

225g (8oz) plain flour

75g (3oz) ground almonds

1. Put the pears and lemon juice into a bowl, add 100g (3½oz) sugar and the mixed spice, then add the blackberries and toss thoroughly to coat.

2. Preheat the oven to 200°C (180°C fan oven) mark 6. Lightly butter a 1.8 litre (3¼ pint) shallow ovenproof dish, then carefully tip the fruit into the dish in an even layer.

3. To make the crumble topping, rub the butter into the flour in a large bowl by hand. Stir in the ground almonds and the remaining sugar. Bring parts of the mixture together with your hands to make lumps.

4. Spoon the crumble topping evenly over the fruit, then put into the oven and bake for 35–45 minutes until the fruit is tender and the crumble is golden and bubbling. Serve with cream, custard or ice cream.

TOP TIP

Crumble is a great way to use leftover, slightly overripe fruit. Replace the pears with apples, or omit the blackberries and use 700g (1½lb) plums or rhubarb instead. You could also use gooseberries (omit the spice), or try 450g (1lb) rhubarb with 450g (1lb) strawberries.

STAR QUALITIES

Comfort food
Share with friends

Express Apple Tart

Serves 8 • Preparation Time 10 minutes • Cooking Time 20 minutes • Per Serving 197 calories, 12g fat (of which 0g saturates), 23g carbohydrate, 0.4g salt • Easy

375g pack ready-rolled puff pastry
500g (1lb 2oz) dessert apples, such
as Cox's, cored and thinly sliced,
then tossed in the juice of
1 lemon (see Top Tip, page 229)
golden icing sugar to dust

1. Preheat the oven to 200°C (180°C fan oven) mark 6. Put the pastry on a 28 x 38cm (11 x 15in) baking sheet and lightly roll over it with a rolling pin to smooth down the pastry. Score lightly around the edge, leaving a 3cm (1¼in) border.

2. Put the apple slices on top of the pastry within the border. Turn the edge of the pastry halfway over to reach the edge of the apples, press down and use your fingers to crimp the edge.

3. Dust heavily with icing sugar. Bake for 20 minutes or until the pastry is cooked and the sugar has caramelised. Serve warm, dusted with more icing sugar.

STAR QUALITIES
Five ingredients or fewer
Cheap eat
Comfort food
Share with friends

Bread & Butter Pudding

Serves 4 • Preparation Time 10 minutes, plus soaking • Cooking Time 30–40 minutes • Per Serving 450 calories, 13g fat (of which 5g saturates), 70g carbohydrate, 1.1g salt • Easy

50g (2oz) unsalted butter, softened, plus extra to grease

275g (10oz) white farmhouse bread, cut into 1cm (½in) slices, crusts removed

50g (2oz) raisins or sultanas

3 medium eggs

450ml (¾ pint) milk

3 tbsp golden icing sugar, plus extra to dust

1. Lightly butter four 300ml (½ pint) gratin dishes or one 1.1 litre (2 pint) ovenproof dish. Butter the bread, then cut into quarters to make triangles. Arrange the bread in the dish(es) and sprinkle with the raisins or sultanas.

2. Beat the eggs, milk and sugar in a bowl. Pour the mixture over the bread and leave to soak for 10 minutes. Preheat the oven to 180°C (160°C fan oven) mark 4.

3. Put the pudding(s) in the oven and bake for 30–40 minutes. Dust with icing sugar to serve.

Three Quick Sauces for Ice Cream

The Best Chocolate Sauce

Put 75g (3oz) roughly chopped plain chocolate into a small heatproof bowl set over a pan of simmering water, making sure the base of the bowl doesn't touch the water. Pour in 150ml (¼ pint) double cream, then leave the chocolate to melt over very low heat. It will take about 10 minutes. Don't stir, or it will thicken to a sticky mess. Once melted, gently stir until smooth. Serve with ice cream or poached pears.

TRY SOMETHING DIFFERENT

Add a shot of espresso coffee to the cream and chocolate while they're melting together.
Use mint-flavoured chocolate instead of plain.

Butterscotch Sauce

Heat 50g (2oz) butter, 50g (2oz) golden caster sugar, 75g (3oz) light muscovado sugar and 150g (5oz) golden syrup together gently, stirring, until melted. Cook for 5 minutes, then remove from the heat. Stir in 125ml (4fl oz) double cream, a few drops of vanilla extract and the juice of ½ lemon and stir over a low heat for 1–2 minutes.

Strawberry Sauce

Put 225g (8oz) hulled strawberries and 2–3 tbsp icing sugar in a blender and whiz well to combine. Alternatively, mash well with a fork or potato masher. Sieve the sauce and chill until needed.

STAR QUALITIES

Ready in under 30 minutes
Quick and easy
Comfort food
Share with friends

Index